YOUR ULTIMATE VICTORY

VICTORY SERIES

STUDY **8**

YOUR ULTIMATE VICTORY

STAND STRONG IN THE FAITH

NEIL T. ANDERSON

BETHANYHOUSE

a division of Baker Publishing Group
www.BethanyHouse.com

Published by Bethany House Publishers
11400 Hampshire Avenue South
Bloomington, Minnesota 55438
www.bethanyhouse.com

Bethany House Publishers is a division of
Baker Publishing Group, Grand Rapids, Michigan

Printed in the United States of America

Library of Congress Control Number: 2014958633

ISBN 978-0-7642-1705-0

Cover design by Rob Williams, InsideOutCreativeArts

15   16   17   18   19   20   21   7   6   5   4   3   2   1

Contents

Contents

Introduction

The Victory Series

S o then, just as you received Christ Jesus as Lord, continue to live your lives in him, rooted and built up in him, strengthened in the faith as you were taught" (Colossians 2:6–7). Paul's New Covenant theology is based on who we are "in Christ." As a believer in Christ, you must first be rooted "in Him" so you can be built up "in Him." Just as you encounter challenges as you grow physically, you will encounter hurdles as you grow spiritually. The following chart illustrates what obstacles you need to overcome and lessons you need to learn at various stages of growth spiritually, rationally, emotionally, volitionally, and relationally.

Levels of Conflict

	Level One Rooted in Christ	Level Two Built up in Christ	Level Three Living in Christ
Spiritual	Lack of salvation or assurance (Eph. 2:1–3)	Living according to the flesh (Gal. 5:19–21)	Insensitive to the Spirit's leading (Heb. 5:11–14)
Rational	Pride and ignorance (1 Cor. 8:1)	Wrong belief or philosophy (Col. 2:8)	Lack of knowledge (Hos. 4:6)
Emotional	Fearful, guilty, and shameful (Matt. 10:26–33; Rom. 3:23)	Angry, anxious, and depressed (Eph. 4:31; 1 Pet. 5:7; 2 Cor. 4:1–18)	Discouraged and sorrowful (Gal. 6:9)

	Level One Rooted in Christ	**Level Two** Built up in Christ	**Level Three** Living in Christ
Volitional	Rebellious (1 Tim. 1:9)	Lack of self-control (1 Cor. 3:1–3)	Undisciplined (2 Thess. 3:7, 11)
Relational	Rejected and unloved (1 Pet. 2:4)	Bitter and unforgiving (Col. 3:13)	Selfish (1 Cor. 10:24; Phil. 2:1–5)

This VICTORY SERIES will address these obstacles and hurdles and help you understand what it means to be firmly rooted in Christ, grow in Christ, live free in Christ, and overcome in Christ. The goal of the course is to help you attain greater levels of spiritual growth, as the following diagram illustrates:

Levels of Growth

	Level One Rooted in Christ	**Level Two** Built up in Christ	**Level Three** Living in Christ
Spiritual	Child of God (Rom. 8:16)	Lives according to the Spirit (Gal. 5:22–23)	Led by the Spirit (Rom. 8:14)
Rational	Knows the truth (John 8:32)	Correctly uses the Bible (2 Tim. 2:15)	Adequate and equipped (2 Tim. 3:16–17)
Emotional	Free (Gal. 5:1)	Joyful, peaceful, and patient (Gal. 5:22)	Contented (Phil. 4:11)
Volitional	Submissive (Rom. 13:1–5)	Self-controlled (Gal. 5:23)	Disciplined (1 Tim. 4:7–8)
Relational	Accepted and forgiven (Rom. 5:8; 15:7)	Forgiving (Eph. 4:32)	Loving and unselfish (Phil. 2:1–5)

God's Story for You and *Your New Identity*, the first two studies in the VICTORY SERIES, focused on the issues that help the believer become firmly rooted in Christ (level one in above chart). If you have completed those studies, then you know the whole gospel, who you are in Christ, and who your heavenly Father is. The four subsequent studies—*Your Foundation in Christ, Renewing Your Mind, Growing in Faith,* and *Your Life in Christ*—discussed issues related to your spiritual growth and what it means to live and minister to others in Christ (level two and three in the above chart).

Introduction

The final two studies in the series—*Your Authority in Christ*, and this study, *Your Ultimate Victory*—examine the enemies of our sanctification and how to overcome the world, the flesh, and the devil. As you work through the six sessions in this Bible study, you will learn how Satan attempts to influence your mind and how he tries to lure people with false knowledge and power. You will explore the tactics he has used from the beginning and how you can overcome his temptations, accusations, and deceptions. You will discover how to identify false teachers and false prophets and how to resist demonic influence, possession, bondage, and control.

Building your life on Christ requires the right foundation, which is your personal identity and security in Christ. For this reason, the Steps to Freedom in Christ will be mentioned during this study. This booklet can be purchased at any Christian bookstore or from Freedom in Christ Ministries. The Steps to Freedom in Christ is a repentance process that can help you resolve your personal and spiritual conflicts. The theology and application of the Steps is explained in the book *Discipleship Counseling*.

Before starting each daily reading, review the portion of Scripture listed for that day, then complete the questions at the end of each day's reading. These questions have been written to allow you to reflect on the material and apply to your life the ideas presented in the reading. At the end of each study, I have included a quote from a Church father illustrating the continuity of the Christian faith. Featured articles will appear in the text throughout the series, which are for the edification of the reader and not necessarily meant for discussion.

If you are part of a small group, be prepared to share your thoughts and insights with your group. You may also want to set up an accountability partnership with someone in your group to encourage you as you apply what you have learned in each session. For those of you who are leading a small group, there are leader tips at the end of this book that will help you guide your participants through the material.

As with any spiritual discipline, you will be tempted at times not to finish this study. There is a "sure reward" for those who make a "sure commitment." The VICTORY SERIES is far more than an intellectual exercise. The truth will not set you free if you only acknowledge it and discuss it on an intellectual level. For the truth to transform your life, you must believe it personally and allow it to sink deep into your heart. Trust the Holy Spirit to lead you into all truth, and enable you to be the person God has created you to be. Decide to live what you have chosen to believe.

Dr. Neil T. Anderson

The Battle for Our Minds

For years, ever since I was a teenager (I am now thirty-six), I heard "voices" in my head. There were four in particular and sometimes what seemed like loud choruses of them. When the subject of schizophrenia would come up on television or in a magazine, I would say to myself, "I know I'm not schizophrenic, but what is this in my head?" I was tortured, mocked, and jeered. Every single thought I had was second-guessed. Consequently, I had zero self-esteem. I often used to wish the voices would be quiet, and I always wondered if other people had them as well. Was this common?

When I started to learn about taking every thought captive in obedience to Christ, and when I read about other people's experiences with these voices, I came to recognize them for what they were. I was able to make them leave, and it was an amazing and beautiful thing to be fully quiet in my mind after so many years of torment. I do not need to explain further all the wonderful things that came with this mental freedom. It has been a true blessing.

—anonymous testimony

Daily Readings

1. Deceptive Thoughts	1 Chronicles 21:1–17
2. Satan's Schemes	2 Corinthians 2:1–11
3. Led Astray	2 Corinthians 11:1–13
4. Deceiving Spirits	1 Timothy 3:14–4:5
5. Mental Illness	Daniel 4:1–37

1

Deceptive Thoughts

1 Chronicles 21:1–17

Key Point

To whoever or whatever we yield ourselves, by that we will be controlled.

Key Verse

The devil . . . was a murderer from the beginning, not holding to the truth, for there is no truth in him. When he lies, he speaks his native language, for he is a liar and the father of lies.

John 8:44

Christians all over the world are struggling with tempting, condemning, and mocking thoughts. Where are those thoughts coming from? Do we personally come up with such thoughts as a means of self-torture or loathing? Is this just self-talk, or could we be paying attention to a deceiving spirit, which Paul warned about in 1 Timothy 4:1: "The Spirit clearly says that in later times some will abandon the faith and follow deceiving spirits and things taught by demons"?

The fact that Satan is capable of putting thoughts in our minds is clearly taught in Scripture. It was recorded in 1 Chronicles 21:1 that "Satan rose up against Israel and incited David to take a census of Israel." What is wrong with taking a census? Shouldn't David know the strength of his military? This passage reveals the subtle nature of Satan and his strategies. Satan knew that David had a whole heart for God and would not willingly or knowingly defy the Lord. Satan's strategy was to get David to put his confidence in *his resources* rather than *God's resources*, which is a major issue to this day. Joab knew it was wrong and tried to stop David, but the king overruled him (see verses 3–4). Thousands died as a result of David's sin.

How did Satan incite David? Did he talk audibly to him? No, the idea for the census came from David's mind—it was his idea, or at least he thought it was. Therein lies the deception. Deceiving thoughts often come "first person singular" in such a way that we think they are our thoughts. If we knew the true source of them, then we would no longer be deceived.

The origin of negative "self-talk" could certainly be our old nature or the world, but that was not the case for Judas. "During supper, the devil having already put into the heart of Judas Iscariot, the son of Simon, to betray Him" (John 13:2 NASB). We may be tempted to think this was just a bad decision prompted by the flesh, but that is not what Scripture says. Being a thief is probably what made Judas vulnerable, but it doesn't explain from where the idea came. When Judas realized that he had been deceived, he took his own life (see Matthew 27:5).

In the earliest days of the Church, God struck down Ananias and Sapphira because they had kept back half of their property and allowed the Church community to think they had given it all (see Acts 5:1–2, 5–10). The judgment seems rather severe for the crime, but Peter reveals why the Lord intervened: "Ananias, how is it that Satan has so filled your heart that you have lied to the Holy Spirit?" (Acts 5:3). God had to send a powerful message to the Early Church, because He knew what the real battle was.

If Satan and his demons can deceive us into believing a lie, they can exert some control over our lives with disastrous results. Any lie we believe, regardless of its source, will have a negative effect on how we live. To whoever or whatever we yield ourselves, by that we shall be controlled. The word "filled" in Acts 5:3 is the same word used in Ephesians 5:18, where we are admonished to be "filled" with the Holy Spirit. This strategy is not new. Eve was deceived and she believed a lie.

What evidence from Scripture do we have that shows Satan is capable of putting thoughts in our minds?

How can believing lies have a negative impact on our personal lives, our marriages, our families, and our ministries?

In Acts 5:1–10, why did God strike down Ananias and Sapphira? What does it mean to be filled?

Which would be worse for you: having a neurological mental illness, or being deceived by an evil spirit? Which would be easier to resolve? Explain.

Why do you think the Western Church readily accepts the diagnosis and explanation of secular psychology and psychiatry and struggles to believe what Scripture teaches about spiritual deception?

_____

_____

_____

It was not on account of this accusation that Peter gave such a severe sentence to the transgressors [Ananias and Sapphira], but in the Spirit he foresaw future weeds that would by their deformed character adulterate the simplicity of the church. . . . He did not allow the culprits to be healed by any repentance, but in order to strike fear into the generations to come, he took care to cut the noxious shoot out by the roots.

Bede (AD 673–735)

2

Satan's Schemes

2 Corinthians 2:1–11

Key Point

A root of bitterness will defile many people.

Key Verse

But their minds [noema] were made dull, for to this day the same veil remains when the old covenant is read. It has not been removed, because only in Christ is it taken away.

2 Corinthians 3:14

In previous studies in the VICTORY SERIES, we explored how mental strongholds/flesh patterns/defense mechanisms are developed in our minds before we come to Christ. Now let's consider the second half of 2 Corinthians 10:5: "We take captive every thought [*noema*] to make it obedient to Christ." The verb is present tense. In one sense it doesn't make any difference whether the thoughts are coming from our old nature, from the world, or from the father of lies. We examine every thought, and if it is not true, we don't think it—and we certainly don't believe it.

The word *noema* only occurs about six times in Scripture, of which five are in this epistle. It has been translated as "thought," "mind" and "schemes." The way in which the word is used is revealing and helps clarify what it means. Paul wrote concerning the need to forgive, "I have forgiven in the sight of Christ for your sake, in order that Satan might not outwit us. For we are not unaware of his schemes [*noema*]" (2 Corinthians 2:10–11). We will not be able to set captives free or heal the wounded without helping them forgive others as Christ has forgiven them. Satan will take advantage of our bitterness. We are cautioned not to let a root of bitterness spring up causing trouble and defiling many (see Hebrews 12:15). Wounds that are not healed are transferred.

Concerning salvation, Paul wrote, "[Satan] has blinded the minds [*noema*] of unbelievers, so that they cannot see the light of the gospel that displays the glory of Christ, who is the image of God" (2 Corinthians 4:4; see also 3:14, in which "minds" is also *noema*). Those who live under the law and cannot see their need for Christ have had their minds blinded by Satan. We would understand the need for prayer and pray differently if we understood how Satan blinds the minds or thoughts of unbelievers. Evangelism was more effective in the Early Church when they understood how to free people from demonic influences. Being able to do so became a test of righteousness and orthodoxy.

For the fifth usage of *noema* in this epistle, Paul wrote, "I am afraid that just as Eve was deceived by the serpent's cunning, your minds [*noema*] may somehow be led astray from your sincere and pure devotion to Christ" (11:3). Satan deceived Eve, and she believed his lies. The temptation is to believe that if we are nice people, such deception can't happen to us, but Eve was *sinless* at the time she was deceived. Good people can be deceived. Notice the spiritual context every time Paul uses the word *noema* in 2 Corinthians.

The final use of the word *noema* is found in Philippians 4:6–7: "Do not be anxious about anything [i.e., don't be double-minded], but in every situation, by prayer and petition, with thanksgiving, present your requests to God. And the peace of God, which transcends all understanding, will guard your hearts and your minds [*noema*] in Christ Jesus." In order to stand against Satan's mental assaults, we must choose to think on "whatever is true, whatever is noble, whatever is right, whatever is pure, whatever is lovely, whatever is admirable—if anything is excellent or praiseworthy—think about such things" (verse 8). Then we must put our righteous thoughts into practice, "and the God of peace will be with [us]" (verse 9).

How should we understand the usage of the word *noema* in 2 Corinthians?

How can believers exercise their authority over the kingdom of darkness to pray for unbelievers?

How do we know that even a good person can be deceived? If good people can be deceived, how else can we protect ourselves?

How can you know if your thoughts are true or not?

How can you become single-minded?

_____

_____

_____

Satan can destroy even under the show of piety. For he can destroy not only by leading into fornication but even by the opposite, the immoderate sorrow which can follow on repentance for it. To take us by sin is his proper work, but to ensnare us in our repentance is an even more subtle disgrace, because that is our weapon, not his.

John Chrysostom (AD 347–407)

3

Led Astray

2 Corinthians 11:1–13

Key Point

Those who have the wrong Jesus have a different spirit and a different gospel.

Key Verses

Satan himself masquerades as an angel of light. It is not surprising, then, if his servants also masquerade as servants of righteousness.

2 Corinthians 11:14–15

Paul had discovered that false prophets had invaded the Corinthian church. He was concerned that comparing his own ministry with that of the false prophets could appear as foolish boasting. He expressed his main concern, however, in verse 3: "But I am afraid that just as Eve was deceived by the serpent's cunning, your minds may somehow be led astray from your sincere and pure devotion to Christ."

The basis for Paul's concern was that these false prophets in the church were talking about the same historical Jesus but were preaching Him a different way. He wrote, "For if someone comes to you and preaches a Jesus other than the Jesus we preached, or if you receive a different spirit from the Spirit you received, or a different gospel from the one you accepted, you put up with it easily enough" (verse 4).

Christology is the primary doctrine that separates Christianity from the cults. Orthodox Christianity asserts that Jesus is the Son of God, the second Person of the Trinity, the promised Messiah, who was one Person with two natures (fully God and fully man). Jesus said, "I told you that you would die in your sins; if you do not believe that I am he, you will indeed die in your sins" (John 8:24).

To believe in Jesus wrongly is to receive a different spirit. If what we have received is not the Holy Spirit, it can only be an evil spirit. Demons, like their leader, can masquerade as angels of light. These spirit guides will seldom reveal their true nature as long as we continue to believe a lie. Such demons are behind cults, which do the work of Satan as the cult leaders masquerade as servants of righteousness. Consequently, many cult members can appear to live righteous lives. Their beliefs are typically legalistic and their leadership extremely authoritarian.

If you have the wrong Jesus and the wrong spirit, you will have the wrong gospel. If Jesus isn't who He said He is, then His sacrifice is not efficacious. His sacrificial death would be no different from the sacrifice of bulls and goats, which do not take away sin (see Hebrews 10:4). An erroneous gospel is not the gospel of grace but a false gospel of works. If we believe that Jesus did not die for the sins of humankind—as some cults teach—then we can be led to believe we must perform good works or religious services in order to receive forgiveness and eternal life.

At the other extreme, New Age philosophies see Jesus as the master psychic. New Agers believe that He had the "spiritual power" to see and hear things that others could not, and they seek that power and enlightenment through mediums and spirit guides. New Age practitioners say we don't need a Messiah to die for our sins—we just need to be enlightened to the truth that we are gods. They have bought the original lie that Satan sold to Eve. In John 7, when Jesus taught in the Temple courts and revealed what was in the people's hearts, the crowd answered, "You are demon-possessed" (verse 20). They knew what He said was true, but they believed that He was getting His information from demons, just like modern-day psychics.

In 2 Corinthians 11:1–13, what was Paul's main concern for the believers?

_____

_____

_____

What separates Christianity from cults?

_____

_____

_____

If someone had esoteric (special) knowledge during the time of Christ, the people assumed he or she was getting the information from demons. What can we learn from this?

_____

_____

_____

What cults are you aware of that don't have orthodox teaching about Jesus? Do they have a gospel of grace or works?

_____

_____

_____

How cult-proof are you and the church you attend? How easy would it be for you and your church to be deceived?

The serpent deceived Eve by lying to her about God, saying that God merely threatened men with death but would never actually kill anyone. Likewise, the false prophets in Paul's day were saying that the gospel was merely added to the Old Testament and that it was therefore necessary to go on keeping the law of Moses as before. In our own time, there are those who claim that hell is merely a threat, either because it does not exist at all or because it is not an eternal punishment—notions which are contrary to the teaching of Scripture.

Pelagius (AD 390–418)

4

Deceiving Spirits

1 Timothy 3:14–4:5

Key Point

It is the unique work of the Holy Spirit to shed light on the finished work of Christ.

Key Verse

Let the wicked forsake their ways and the unrighteous their thoughts.

Isaiah 55:7

Paul, after speaking about the Church of the living God—the pillar and foundation of truth—inserts a parenthetical remark about the historical visit of Jesus on earth (see 1 Timothy 3:16). Then he says, "The Spirit clearly says that in later times some will abandon the faith and follow deceiving spirits and things taught by demons" (4:1).

Paul's parenthetical insertion in 1 Timothy 3:16 was to draw attention to Christ, which is the major work of the Holy Spirit (see John 16:14). Christians believe deeply in the ministry of the Holy Spirit. If there were no Holy Spirit, there would be no life, no power to live, no gifts, no guidance, no assurance, and no Church. However, we are to be Christ-centered, not spirit-centered. We are to be truth-based, not experienced-based.

"The Spirit" is to be contrasted with "deceiving spirits." There is only one Holy Spirit, but there are many deceiving spirits who are demons or evil spirits. Paul is not telling us by way of parables or by signs and wonders; he is clearly saying there is a coming apostasy in the later days. Concerning the end times, Jesus said, "For false messiahs and false prophets will appear and perform great signs and wonders to deceive, if possible, even the elect. See, I have told you ahead of time" (Matthew 24:24–25; see also 2 Peter 2:1–12).

Psychiatrists, psychologists, counselors, social workers, and pastors routinely work with people who are struggling with their thoughts, are having difficulty concentrating, or are hearing voices. Many cannot read their Bibles or concentrate when they pray or worship God. The voices are usually condemning or blasphemous. Such voices and thoughts cannot be fully explained as a neurological condition or a chemical imbalance.

How can a chemical produce a personality or create a thought that we are opposed to thinking? Is there a natural explanation for this? Why not believe what Scripture has taught and then take the appropriate measures to correct the problem? If the condemning, lying, and blasphemous thoughts leave after we submit to God and resist the devil (see James 4:7), then the origin of the thoughts is not natural or neurological. Believers all over the world have found such relief from oppressive thoughts through genuine repentance (see the Steps to Freedom in Christ). The peace of God is now guarding their hearts and their minds in Christ Jesus (see Philippians 4:7).

Doctrines of demons "come through hypocritical liars, whose consciences have been seared as with a hot iron" (1 Timothy 4:2). They profess to believe one thing but live another way. They have no conscience. They are modern-day Gnostics who advocate an ascetic form of life (see Colossians 2:16–23). Their message is abstinence from things such as marriage and food, but Paul counters by saying, "For everything God created is good, and nothing is to be rejected if it is received with thanksgiving" (1 Timothy 4:4).

Food is the "enemy" for those who struggle with eating disorders. Why do they defecate, binge and purge, and even cut themselves? Because they believe there is evil present within them (see Romans 7:21), but their efforts to rid themselves of that evil are fruitless. Only the shed blood of the Lord Jesus Christ can cleanse them from sin. It is all deception, and only truth can set them free.

What was the purpose of Paul's parenthetical remark in 1 Timothy 3:16?

_____

_____

_____

What is the difference between being Christ-centered and being spirit-centered?

_____

_____

_____

Has the Church in general heeded the warnings about the coming apostasy?

_____

_____

_____

Why do you think the Church has been more interested about the politics and timing of Christ's return and less interested about the warnings about deceiving spirits, false teachers, false prophets, and false Messiahs?

_____

_____

_____

How sharp is your discernment?

_____

_____

_____

They are truly called prophets. . . . Past events and events now taking place compel us to agree with what was spoken by them. Furthermore they deserved to be believed because of the miracles which they performed, since they were glorifying God the Creator and Father of the universe and they were announcing the Christ coming from Him, His Son. The false prophets who were filled with the deceitful and filthy spirit never did nor now do this. They dare to work various supposed miracles in order to impress men, and they glorify the spirits and demons of deceit.

Justin Martyr (AD 100–165)

5

Mental Illness

Daniel 4:1–37

Key Point

Mental illness is a distorted concept of God and a distorted concept of who we are.

Key Verse

The end of all things is near. Therefore be alert and of sober mind so that you may pray.

1 Peter 4:7

God warned Nebuchadnezzar in a dream and Daniel encouraged him to repent (Daniel 4:5–27), but twelve months later he was as proud as ever (see verses 28–30). Finally, he raised his eyes toward heaven, and his sanity was restored (see verse 34). Was he mentally ill? Today's mental health workers would conclude that he was, because they believe people are mentally healthy if they are in touch with reality and relatively free from anxiety. Based on secular standards and definitions, anyone experiencing a spiritual battle for his or her mind would fail on both counts.

What would secular mental health workers think if their clients told them that they were hearing voices or seeing things that frightened them, but the counselors couldn't see or hear anything? They would conclude that their clients were out of touch with reality. Actually, the mental health workers may be the ones out of touch with reality. The ultimate reality is God, and what their clients are seeing and hearing is very real, though not seen and heard through the natural senses.

In the natural realm we can't physically hear anything unless there is a sound source that sends an audible signal through the medium of air to our eardrums. The eardrums pass the signals to our brains. In the same way, we can't physically see anything unless there is a light source sending a light ray that reflects off a material object to our optic nerve, which then sends a signal to our brains. There is no physical source of light and sound in the spiritual realm: "For our struggle is not against flesh and blood" (Ephesians 6:12). The battle is in the mind. Therefore, a spiritual attack that is "seen" or "heard" by one person will probably not be seen or heard by another person in the same setting.

The battle for the mind is tearing families apart. A child cries out at night, "Mommy, there is something in my room!" Most parents will look under the bed and in the closet and say, "Honey, there is nothing here. Go back to sleep." If you saw something in your room, would you go back to sleep? Or a mother comes home from the hospital with her third child. The kids are fighting, her electrolytes are depleted, and she suddenly has a thought: *Kill your kids!* Who is she going to share that thought with? Her husband? "Honey, I've had thoughts about killing the kids!" When people have such thoughts they generally don't kill their kids, but in rare occasions they actually do. Those who don't are disgusted with themselves for even thinking such things.

Such battles for the mind are happening in every church. So why don't we know more about this spiritual battle? First, because we can't read each other's minds, so we have no idea what another person's struggle is unless they have the courage to tell us. Second, because few people are willing to disclose what is going on inside their minds. If one person had the courage to share but others dismiss it, nobody else will ever share again. Third, because some fear they are losing their minds, and they don't want others thinking that they are. Fourth, because some are embarrassed with the thoughts they are having, which may be vulgar, sensual, or just plain evil. All this chaos, and it is just a lie.

In the story told in Daniel 4, how do we know that Nebuchadnezzar's mental illness was spiritual in nature?

How is what we see and hear in the physical realm different from what see and hear in the spiritual realm?

Why aren't people more open about disclosing what their thought life is like?

Would you be willing to disclose to others what your thought life is like? Why or why not?

God knows the thoughts and intentions of our hearts. Why do you think He has kept us from having that ability?

Because the devil was the first to be locked into sin, everyone who now sins acts according to his bidding. For the devil rules in the sinner by a mass of evil thoughts, as in the case of Judas. Someone might say that the devil is present in sinners even before they sin because they have made room for him. The answer to this is that committing sin and making room for the devil amount to one and the same thing—sin.

John Chrysostom (AD 347–407)

Dreams and Nightmares

A mother visited her daughter on the mission field and became sick with malaria. Her body temperature rose to more than 105 degrees, and she started to hallucinate. Later, back in the States, she attended a Discipleship Counseling conference and asked if her hallucinations were demonic. "What were you hallucinating?" she was asked. The woman replied, "Donald Duck, Pluto, and Mickey Mouse." She had spent two days at Disneyland before her trip to Asia.

What this woman experienced was a natural process similar to dreams. When we go to sleep at night, our brain continues to operate and has access to stored information. The normal dreams we experience while sleeping typically consist of people we know and places we have been. The story can be rather creative, but the players and places have already been stored in our memory banks. If a child watches a horror movie in the afternoon and has a nightmare that night, chances are the nightmare will include the characters in the movie. If we put garbage in, then garbage comes out.

On the other hand, terrifying dreams with grotesque images and demonic figures that we have never seen in the natural realm can't be coming from stored memory. It is also highly unlikely that our brains spontaneously create such images against our will. When inquirers report such night terrors, they need to be led through the Steps to Freedom in Christ. The nighttime terrors end when they submit to God through genuine repentance and resist the devil (see James 4:7).

The spiritual source of dreams can also be God, as it was for Nebuchadnezzar. However, in such cases the dreams will always be true and lead to a healthy fear of the Lord, not a debilitating fear that excludes faith in God. So, before you put too much stock in the content of dreams, consider the words of Jeremiah: "Let the prophet who has a dream recount the dream, but let the one who has my word speak it faithfully. For what has straw to do with grain?" (23:28).

The Lure of Knowledge and Power

God showed me that I had been having similar dreams since third grade—dreams that I had met the devil and he had put a curse on me. I asked the Lord what happened in the third grade, and I remembered that I had started watching *Bewitched*. It was my favorite TV show, and I watched it religiously.

Because of that show, I became interested in spiritual powers. Along with many of my school friends, I read books on ghosts, ESP, palm reading, and even a book on spells and curses. It was an "in" thing to play with Magic 8 Balls, Ouija boards, and magic sets. Another favorite show was *Gilligan's Island*, where I got the idea to use my dolls as voodoo dolls to get back at my mother. I considered putting a curse on her. By the time I was in sixth grade, I was so depressed. I started reading Edgar Allan Poe, and it became the only thing I craved.

In high school, the dreams came back and I became suicidal. By the grace of God, I invited Jesus Christ into my life. The biggest thing God showed me when I later went through the Steps to Freedom in Christ was that I knew when I was young that there was evil power out there, and I had desired to have it. This wasn't hocus-pocus to me anymore. I prayed all the prayers and renounced all the lies that had been going on in my family for years. I acknowledged my own sin and lack of forgiveness.

You know how it is when somebody has been in a cult for a long time and they get taken in for deprogramming? That's the way it was for me. It was like God locked me in a room and said, "Give me your brain. We're not leaving until you do." It took an intensive week for me to see the lies in which I had been living. I had no idea.

—anonymous testimony

Daily Readings

1. Counterfeit Christianity	Deuteronomy 18:9–16
2. Esoteric Knowledge	Isaiah 8:19–22
3. Spiritual Demise	1 Samuel 28:1–25
4. The Rise of the New Age	Acts 8:4–25
5. Counterfeit Gifts	Exodus 8:16–19

1

Counterfeit Christianity

Deuteronomy 18:9–16

Key Point

The only One who can perfectly know the future is the One who has the necessary attributes to bring it about.

Key Verses

For false messiahs and false prophets will appear and perform great signs and wonders to deceive, if possible, even the elect. See, I have told you ahead of time.

Matthew 24:24–25

The thirst for knowledge and power has seduced the naïve and undiscerning since the dawn of history. More people have their palms and tea leaves read or read the astrological column in the paper than read the Bible. People want to know the future for various reasons, but the shrewd ones know that knowledge is power.

Just imagine the power you would have if you had "precognition"—if you knew events before they happened. You could become a billionaire just by betting at the racetrack or become politically powerful by accurately predicting future events. In order to accurately predict future events, you would need the power and means to arrange them. God can do that because He is omnipotent and omniscient, which is why the predictions of true prophets are always fulfilled.

Satan has a limited capacity to arrange the future by manipulating people who pay attention to his deceiving spirits. Everything he does is a counterfeit of Christianity. Precognition is a counterfeit of prophecy. Clairvoyance, which is the power to see what the normal five senses cannot see, is a counterfeit of divine revelation. Telepathy, which is the ability to communicate from one mind to another by extrasensory means, is a counterfeit of prayer. Psychokinesis, which is the manipulation of physical matter without the use of physical means, is a counterfeit of God's miracles. Spirit guides, or deceiving spirits, are counterfeits of divine guidance. Why would people want a spirit guide if they could have the Holy Spirit as their guide?

These finite longings for the infinite can only be fulfilled by the knowledge and power that come from an intimate relationship with God. Satan tries to pass off his counterfeits as the real thing. He will gain a foothold in our lives if he can lure us into the deceptive world of psychic knowledge and power. Moses' words of warning in Deuteronomy 18:9–12 are as viable today as they were for the Israelites under his leadership: "When you enter the land the LORD your God is giving you, do not learn to imitate the detestable ways of the nations there. Let no one be found among you who . . . practices divination or sorcery, interprets omens, engages in witchcraft, or casts spells, or who is a medium or spiritist, or who consults the dead. Anyone who does these things is detestable to the Lord."

We live in a contemporary Canaan in which it is socially acceptable to consult spiritists, mediums, palm readers, psychic counselors, and horoscopes for guidance and esoteric knowledge. Because Satan has the capacity to deceive the whole world, it is possible for him to arrange future events— but never perfectly. Only God can prophesy something and guarantee that it will come true. This is one way that we can know whether a prophet is true or false. "If what a prophet proclaims in the name of the LORD does not take place or come true, that is a message the LORD has not spoken. That prophet has spoken presumptuously" (Deuteronomy 18:22).

All the false prophets, psychic counselors, and spiritual mediums have superhuman knowledge, but they are getting it from a counterfeiter. However, because they seem to know more than what is humanly possible, a gullible public pays attention to them and is deceived.

Why do people want to know the future?

_____

_____

_____

How are Satan's ploys a counterfeit of Christianity?

_____

_____

_____

How is a true prophet different from one of Satan's counterfeiters?

_____

_____

_____

Have you ever been tempted to seek psychic powers? What good could come from it?

_____

_____

_____

_____

Do you think any mortal is mature enough to have supernatural knowledge and power without abusing it? Why or why not?

An angel of light is one who is free to speak because he stands close to God. This is what the devil pretends to be.

John Chrysostom (AD 347–407)

Nothing but the mercy of God can save a man from mistaking bad demons for good angels, and false friends for true ones, and from suffering the full damages of this diabolical deception, which is all the more deadly in that it is wily beyond words.

Augustine of Hippo (AD 354–430)

2

Esoteric Knowledge

Isaiah 8:19–22

Key Point

God will cut off from His people those who seek false guidance.

Key Verse

Let us purify ourselves from everything that contaminates body and spirit, perfecting holiness out of reverence for God.

2 Corinthians 7:1

The craving for esoteric or "extra" knowledge has led many people to seek out mediums and spiritists, which God strictly forbids. "Do not turn to mediums or seek out spiritists, for you will be defiled by them. I am the LORD your God" (Leviticus 19:31). God is not restricting us from having knowledge that we need; He has made Himself and His ways known so that we can live productive lives. Sadly, some people don't want to take the time to seek God and study His Word.

Isaiah wrote, "When someone tells you to consult mediums and spiritists, who whisper and mutter, should not a people inquire of their God? Why consult the dead on behalf of the living? Consult God's instruction and the testimony of warning. If anyone does not speak according to this word, they have no light of dawn" (Isaiah 8:19–20). Not much is known about the biblical terms "medium" and "spiritist." Because "medium" (taken from *ob*, meaning "witch" or "necromancer") is feminine, and "spiritist" (taken from *yidd oni*, from the root "to know") is masculine, some scholars think they are the male and female counterparts of the same role, which is to introduce false guidance.

The Lord does not take lightly those who give false guidance or those who seek it out. "I will set my face against anyone who turns to mediums and spiritists to prostitute themselves by following them, and I will cut them off from their people" (Leviticus 20:6). God takes an even tougher stand against those who would lead his people astray: "A man or woman who is a medium or spiritist among you must be put to death. You are to stone them; their blood will be on their own heads" (verse 27).

We don't stone mediums today because we no longer live under Old Testament theocratic law—we are under Christ's New Covenant. However, our culture tends to make them celebrities, put them on talk shows, and schedule them for entertainment. Late-night television is loaded with psychic hotlines promising divine guidance and spiritual help. Many people—including gullible Christians—have sought their false guidance and found themselves in spiritual bondage. God doesn't want such false guidance to pollute the Church, so He cuts them off. This is not what you want!

Younger Christians naïvely participate in what they think are just harmless parlor games. So they ask the Magic 8 Ball questions or play with the Ouija board, but such games are not harmless. A mother and daughter attended a Discipleship Counseling conference and the mother said on the way home, "I don't think people in our church have these kinds of spiritual problems." The daughter replied, "Mom, when I had a slumber party in our home for my birthday, we were upstairs trying to have a séance. I have been plagued by a voice in my head ever since."

To resolve spiritual conflicts arising from false guidance, it is necessary to renounce all involvement and association with false teachers, false prophets, and any and all cult and occult practices. That includes all vows or pledges made to anyone or anything other than Christ. The need to do this also applies to the children and grandchildren whose ancestors participated in any type of idolatry or false guidance (see Exodus 20:4–5). Paul says, "We have renounced secret and shameful ways; we do not use deception, nor do we distort the word of God" (2 Corinthians 4:2).

Why does God prohibit us from seeking out mediums or spiritists? What may happen to us if we do?

_____

_____

_____

What command did God give the Israelites in the Old Testament about how to deal with those who give or receive false guidance? How serious is this sin?

_____

_____

_____

How does our secular culture treat mediums?

_____

_____

_____

Do you believe books and movies such as the Harry Potter series are harmless fun? Why or why not?

_____

_____

_____

Why do you think some teenage Christians want to play Light as a Feather, Bloody Mary, fantasy games, Magic 8 Ball, and Ouija board and have séances?

_____

_____

_____

He [Satan] invented heresies and schisms to undermine faith, pervert truth and break unity. Unable to keep us in the dark ways of former error, he draws us into a new maze of deceit. He snatches men away from the church itself and, just when they think they have drawn near to the light and escaped the night of the world, he plunges them unawares into a new darkness. Though they do not stand by the gospel and discipline and law of Christ, they call themselves Christians. Though they are walking in darkness, they think they are in the light, through the deceitful flattery of the adversary who, as the apostle said, transforms himself into an angel of light and adorns his ministers as ministers of righteousness. They call night day . . . cunningly to frustrate truth by their lying.

Cyprian (AD 200–258)

3

Spiritual Demise

1 Samuel 28:1–25

Key Point

God never bypasses our minds but works through them.

Key Verses

Saul died because he was unfaithful to the Lord; he did not keep the word of the Lord and even consulted a medium for guidance, and did not inquire of the Lord.

1 Chronicles 10:13–14

Saul had sinned, causing God to turn away from him. After much prodding by Samuel, Saul made a half-hearted attempt at repentance, but it was not complete (1 Samuel 15:24–31). "Now the Spirit of the LORD had departed from Saul, and an evil spirit from the LORD tormented him" (1 Samuel 16:14). Under the Old Covenant, the presence of the Holy Spirit was a temporary gifting, just like God's blessings were conditional. Under the New Covenant, the Holy Spirit takes up residence in those who believe, and God says He will never leave or forsake us.

The evil spirit was not *of* God, but was sent *by* God. God reigns supreme, and He can use Satan and his emissaries as a means to discipline His people, as He did with Saul. He also used the godless nation of Assyria to discipline His people (see Isaiah 10:5–6). Even the Church is advised to turn grossly immoral people over to Satan for the destruction of their flesh so that their souls may be saved (see 1 Corinthians 5:5).

After Samuel died, Saul sought guidance from a medium. Saul had previously purged the nation of mediums and spiritists (see 1 Samuel 28:9), but now he was paying a visit to the witch of Endor. Coming to the witch in disguise, Saul persuaded her to call up Samuel (see verses 11–19). However, the scheme backfired when God permitted Samuel himself to return, which terrified the medium. Samuel foretold the imminent capture of Israel by the Philistines and the death of Saul and his son (see verse 19).

God expressly forbids the practice of necromancy, which is an attempt to bring up the spirits of the dead (see Isaiah 8:19–20). The story of the rich man and Lazarus teaches the present-day impossibility of communicating with the dead (see Luke 16:19–31). When a secular psychologist claims to have regressed a client back to a former state of existence through hypnosis, don't believe it. When a psychic claims to have contacted the dead, don't believe it. When a New Age medium purports to channel a person from the past into the present, realize that it is nothing more than a demonic spirit or the fraudulent work of a con artist.

A lady was once working through the Steps to Freedom when she suddenly became frightened. When the encourager asked what she was hearing or seeing, she said, "You mean you don't see my father standing right there?" The encourager didn't bother to look, because he knew he wouldn't see anything. Instead he asked, "Tell me about your father." She said, "I'm responsible for my father." Of course that was not true, but that was what she had been taught by her father, who was a Mormon. When they started the Steps again she had another apparition of her grandmother, who had introduced the family to Mormonism. The woman became free when she renounced Mormon practices and beliefs.

Mediums have to reach a passive state of the mind in order to channel spirits, which is the most dangerous thing one can do spiritually. God never bypasses our minds; He works through them. Hypnosis also bypasses the conscious use of the mind and is not a practice in which Christians should participate. "Brothers and sisters, stop thinking like children. In regard to evil be infants, but in your thinking be adults" (1 Corinthians 14:20).

What can we learn from the fact that God uses evil spirits, evil people, and nations to accomplish His objectives?

_____

_____

_____

What is wrong with inducing a passive state of mind?

_____

_____

_____

Why was the witch of Endor frightened when she saw Samuel?

_____

_____

_____

What would you say or do if you were being encouraged to assume a passive state of mind or being tempted to take a mind-altering drug?

_____

_____

_____

What would you do if you or someone you were trying to help suddenly had an apparition of a deceased relative?

_____

_____

_____

As we have already suggested, there is hardly a human being who is unattended by a demon. And it is well known to many that premature and violent deaths (which men ascribe to accidents) are in fact brought about by demons. . . . For in cases of exorcism, [the evil spirits] sometimes claim to be one of the relatives of the persons possessed by him. . . . The situation is similar in the other kind of sorcery that is supposed to bring up from Hades the souls now resting there.

Tertullian (AD 160–220)

4

The Rise of the New Age

Acts 8:4–25

Key Point

The New Age movement cloaks the occultic message of enlightenment.

Key Verse

You have no part or share in this ministry, because your heart is not right before God.

Acts 8:21

Since the day of Pentecost, all believers have received the Holy Spirit. Persecution in Jerusalem caused the gospel to spread to surrounding regions. The believers in Samaria had an incomplete gospel, which the apostles now graciously supplied in full (see Acts 8:14–17), and they too received the Holy Spirit. The disciples of Jesus were performing miracles, and evil spirits were coming out of many (see verse 7).

At the same time in Samaria, a man named Simon amazed people with his sorcery. The people called him the "Great Power of God" (verse 10), and they followed him because he amazed them with his magic. However, when they heard the good news from Philip, they believed it. Simon also professed to believe and was even baptized (see verses 12–13), but then he tried to offer money to have the same "magical" power the disciples had—a practice to this day called "simony" (see Acts 8:18–19).

Peter immediately rebuked Simon for thinking that he could buy the gift of God with money. He called for Simon to repent, because he could tell that Simon was full of bitterness and captive to sin, which indicated he was probably not a true believer (see verses 20–23). Obviously, the spiritual battle continued after Pentecost. The thirst for knowledge and power still lures a gullible public to seek false guidance. There are many customers like those in Acts 16:16–18 who sought guidance from a demonized slave girl, and there are many who will make a profit from them.

Although spiritism and various cults and occultic practices have been present in American culture from the beginning, the New Age movement has received much broader participation. Through New Age teachings, materialistic humanism gives way to a new Enlightenment: "You don't need God; you *are* God. You don't need to repent of your sins and depend on God to save you. You just need to be enlightened. So turn off your mind and tune in to the great cosmic oneness through some mystical harmonic convergence." The New Age pitch is the oldest lie of Satan: "You will be like God" (Genesis 3:5). Practitioners change the names from "medium" to "channeler," "demon" to "spirit guide," and a gullible public buys it and spends big money doing so.

The "harlots" of the New Age movement may well represent the mystery religion of Babylon. "With her the kings of the earth committed adultery, and the inhabitants of the earth were intoxicated with the wine of her adulteries" (Revelation 17:2). Every country in the world has opened its doors to paranormal and psychic research. What the rulers of the countries of the world don't know is that they have embraced the religion of the Antichrist—which is masquerading under the guise of science. They have no idea that they are playing right into the hands of Satan.

Such kings are like Jeshurun (a poetic name for Israel): "Jeshurun grew fat and kicked. . . . They abandoned the God who made them and rejected the Rock their Savior. . . . They sacrificed to false gods, which are not

God—gods they had not known, gods that recently appeared, gods your ancestors did not fear. You deserted the Rock, who fathered you; you forgot the God who gave you birth" (Deuteronomy 32:15, 17–18).

According to Acts 8:4–25, what kind of power did Simon have? Where, or from whom, did the people think Simon got his power? What kind of power did he want?

_____

_____

_____

How did Peter see through him?

_____

_____

_____

Although the kings of the earth are not going to embrace any one organized religion, what are they embracing?

_____

_____

_____

What can you say to someone in the New Age movement who believes in Jesus and respects Him as a great psychic?

_____

_____

_____

Have you observed any "Christians" profiting from their miraculous gifts? How would you know if they are legitimate Christian workers?

_____

_____

_____

Simon the magician had been washed indeed in the fount but not clean in his heart; the subsequent punishment revealed him to the world as ignorant of the faith.

Arator (c. sixth century AD)

[Simon] did not say, "Give me also the participation in the Holy Spirit," but "give me this power," with a view to selling to others what could not be sold—something he himself did not possess.

Cyril of Jerusalem (AD 313–386)

5

Counterfeit Gifts

Exodus 8:16–19

Key Point

Satan seeks to counterfeit the spiritual gifts God has given the Church.

Key Verses

Therefore, my brothers and sisters, be eager to prophesy, and do not forbid speaking in tongues. But everything should be done in a fitting and orderly way.

1 Corinthians 14:39–40

Pharaoh of Egypt was not willing to let God's people go, so the Lord sent one plague after another upon the land. It is interesting to note that Pharaoh hardened his own heart several times before the Lord finally hardened it (see Exodus 9:12). He likely could have turned his heart to God at one time, but ultimately he no longer could. This sequential hardening of our own hearts will lead to a depraved mind—a mind devoid of logic that will lead to extreme depravity (see Romans 1:28–32). It wasn't until the tenth plague that Pharaoh finally relented and let God's people go for self-preservation (see Exodus 12:31), but he never repented.

At first Pharaoh summoned his magicians and sorcerers, and they, by their secret arts, were able to mimic what Moses had done (see Exodus 7:11, 22; 8:7). "But when the magicians tried to produce gnats by their secret arts, they could not. . . . The magicians said to Pharaoh, 'This is the finger of God'" (8:18–19). The magicians' powers could only go so far. They could mimic what Moses did until God created gnats out of dust. Satan has no power to create, so the rest of the plagues went unmatched.

The magicians knew it was the finger of God when they couldn't counterfeit what He was doing. Similar spiritual counterfeiters will continue throughout the Church Age, culminating with "terrible times in the last days" (2 Timothy 3:1). "Just as Jannes and Jambres opposed Moses, so also these teachers oppose the truth. They are men of depraved minds, who, as far as the faith is concerned, are rejected" (verse 8).

The magic the sorcerers practiced in the Old Testament is not the same as the entertaining tricks that our modern magicians do. Magicians who seek to entertain us have the ability to create illusions by using clever tricks and sleight of hand. In a similar way, some "psychics" are only doing "cold readings." These clever charlatans ask the naïve a few leading questions. They observe their clients' speech, mannerisms, appearance, and dress. Based on these observations, such "psychics" make general statements that can appear to be accurate. The gullible are so impressed with the accuracy of their "revelations" that they start giving more information, which these charlatans fabricate into a "reading." This is not demonic; it's just verbal sleight of hand. However, it does reveal just how easy it is for people to be deceived.

The mediums and spiritists whom God spoke against in Leviticus and Deuteronomy were not con artists but people who possessed real spiritual power. They were channels for the demonic and knew in their own ranks who the true psychics were. Today, while the charlatans, with their phony cold readings, are only interested in bilking us out of our money, true mediums and spiritists want to enslave us and expand the control of Satan. The evil one will also counterfeit many of the spiritual gifts with which God has endowed the Church. This is especially true of the gifts of tongues and prophecy, which are reported in false religions and in cults around the world. "Dear friends, do not believe every spirit, but test the spirits to see whether they are from God, because many false prophets have gone out into the world" (1 John 4:1).

What may happen if one hardens his or her heart too many times?

Why couldn't Pharaoh's magicians mimic the plague of gnats?

Con artist "psychics" draw their information from people, while spiritual psychics/mediums receive their information from demons. How can you tell the difference?

How can you avoid being conned by clever charlatans who lead people to believe they have true spiritual powers?

How would you respond to a medium who revealed accurate details about your life and had a special message for you from God?

_____

_____

_____

Who is it who tests the spirits, and how can they be tested? Our Lord shows this in the Gospels, where He predicted that evil spirits of the kind of which John had experienced would come. Jesus said, "Beware of false prophets, who come to you in sheep's clothing but inwardly are ravenous wolves. You will know them by their fruits. Are grapes gathered from thorns, or figs from thistles?" These therefore are the fruits by which the evil spirits who speak by false prophets can be discerned: the thorns of schisms and the terrible thistles of heresy which sting all those who go anywhere near them.

Bede (AD 673–735)

Overcoming Temptation

Having devotions with little children can be an exercise in frustration. For the children, it is a contest between the length of their attention span and how long they can sit still. One will precipitate the termination of the other. The challenge for us as the parents is clarity. Our children's "why is this" and "why is that" questions force us to rethink what we really believe and hopefully explain it in a clear and simple way. How well do we understand something if we can't explain it to children? Try explaining temptation to a child when they have a hard time understanding the word "no." But so do adults, because just saying "no" doesn't always work. Remember, the Law has the capacity to stimulate the desire to do what it was intended to prohibit (see Romans 7:5, 8).

Maybe there is something we can learn from children. Have you ever noticed that resisting temptation is easier for children when a parent is present? They give in to temptation when they are alone or with other children who are like-minded. Even a child knows that when the cat is away, the mouse will play. So, when is a true believer ever alone? Is there any time when our Father is not present? How much easier would it be to overcome temptation if we practiced the presence of God? So, when the tempter comes knocking, open up the door of your heart and show him Jesus.

Daily Readings

1. Confronting Temptation	Matthew 4:1–11
2. Lust of the Flesh	Genesis 3:1–7
3. Lust of the Eyes	Deuteronomy 6:4–19
4. The Pride of Life	Proverbs 16:16–24
5. Too Much of a Good Thing	1 Corinthians 6:12–20

1

Confronting Temptation
Matthew 4:1–11

Key Point

In Christ we have the resources to overcome every temptation.

Key Verse

No temptation has overtaken you except what is common to mankind. And God is faithful; he will not let you be tempted beyond what you can bear. But when you are tempted, he will also provide a way out so that you can endure it.

1 Corinthians 10:13

The Holy Spirit led Jesus into the wilderness to be tempted. No human being could have been more vulnerable. Jesus was alone in the wilderness and on the verge of starvation after fasting for forty days. The temptation was directed at His humanity. The goal was to show us how a spiritually alive person could stand up to Satan's temptations in a worst-case scenario. It wasn't a show of superior power; it was an example of humble dependence.

The devil, seeking to take advantage of Jesus' vulnerability, said, "If you are the Son of God, tell these stones to become bread" (Matthew 4:3). Satan wanted Jesus to use His divine attributes independently of God the Father to save Himself. That was essentially the same as Peter's advice to Jesus that prompted His stern rebuke, "Get behind me, Satan!" (16:23). All temptation is an attempt to get us to live our lives independently of God. Jesus responded by declaring His dependence on God the Father: "It is written: 'Man shall not live on bread alone, but on every word that comes from the mouth of God'" (4:4).

Then the devil took Jesus to Jerusalem and stood Him on the highest point of the Temple. "'If you are the Son of God,' he said, 'throw yourself down. For it is written: "He will command his angels concerning you, and they will lift you up in their hands"'" (verse 6). The devil wanted Jesus to test God's Word, but Christ knew we don't put God to the test. He tests us. Finally, the devil took Jesus to a high mountain to show Him the kingdoms of the world. He offered these kingdoms to Jesus if the Lord would only worship him (see verses 8–9). However, Jesus said He would only worship the Lord our God and serve Him only (see verse 10).

John describes three channels of temptation that we will have to face in this world: "For everything in the world—the lust of the flesh, the lust of the eyes, and the pride of life—comes not from the Father but from the world" (1 John 2:16). These were exactly the same for Adam and Eve as they were for Jesus. Adam and Eve failed the test and plunged the whole world into sin, but Jesus passed the test and proved to be the Savior of the world and an example for us to follow. "For we do not have a high priest who is unable to empathize with our weaknesses, but we have one who has been tempted in every way, just as we are—yet he did not sin" (Hebrews 4:15).

As we study these three channels, keep in mind that they are only doors of opportunity that Satan takes advantage of. In Christ we have the resources and the power to conquer every temptation that Satan throws at us. The basis for temptation is legitimate needs that we all have. When we don't perceive that our basic needs are being met, we are much more vulnerable to temptation. God promises to meet all our needs according to his glorious riches in Christ Jesus (see Philippians 4:19). If we know that our lives, identity, acceptance, security, and significance are all found in Christ, we will not be so easily tempted to find them elsewhere.

In Matthew 4:1–11, why did the Holy Spirit lead Jesus into the wilderness after He fasted for forty days?

What should we learn from Jesus' example?

What are the three channels of temptation through which Satan works?

What legitimate needs do you have that tempt you to seek fulfillment in the world as opposed to Christ?

Do you have a dependent or semi-dependent relationship with God? What are the consequences of the latter?

_____

_____

_____

The testimony was taken from Deuteronomy. The Lord responded in this way, for it was His purpose to overcome the devil with humility and not with power. The Savior's very response indicates that it was as man that he was tempted.

Jerome (AD 347–420)

If as God Jesus overcame the devil, it was no great accomplishment for Him to defeat the apostate angel whom He Himself had made. Nor is this victory to be ascribed to His humanity alone. But by long-suffering, He prevailed over him as man, teaching us that it is not through miracles but by long-suffering and patient endurance that we must prevail over the devil and that we should do nothing merely for show or for notoriety's sake.

Theodore of Mopsuestia (AD 350–428)

Channels of Temptation

1 John 2:15–17

	Lust of the flesh (appetites and cravings)	Lust of the eyes (self-interest)	Pride of life (self-promotion)
Eve	"The woman saw that the fruit of the tree was good for food . . ." (Gen. 3:6)	"and pleasing to the eye . . ." (Gen. 3:6)	"and also desirable for gaining wisdom" (Gen. 3:6)
Satan	"Did God really say, 'You must not eat from any tree in the garden'?" (Gen. 3:1)	"You will not certainly die" (Gen. 3:4)	"You will be like God" (Gen. 3:5)
Questions	The will of God (see Gal. 6:8)	The Word of God (see Matt. 16:24–26)	The worship of God (see 1 Pet. 5:5–11)
Destroys	Dependence on God	Confidence in God	Obedience to God
Jesus	"Man does not live on bread alone but on every word that comes from the mouth of the LORD" (Deut. 8:3)	"Do not put the LORD your God to the test" (Deut. 6:16).	"Fear the LORD your God, serve him only" (Deut. 6:13).

2

Lust of the Flesh

Genesis 3:1–7

Key Point

The Word of God is compromised when we succumb to the lust of the flesh.

Key Verses

When tempted, no one should say, "God is tempting me." For God cannot be tempted by evil, nor does he tempt anyone; but each person is tempted when they are dragged away by their own evil desire and enticed.

James 1:13–14

In the Garden of Eden, Satan first appealed to the lust of the flesh. The fruit looked good to Eve, so why not have a bite? "Did God really say, 'You must not eat from any tree in the garden'?" (Genesis 3:1). Notice that the devil said "any tree" when God said only "the tree of the knowledge of good and evil" (2:17). Satan distorts and questions the Word of God when he attacks the mind.

The key to winning the battle for your mind is to recognize tempting thoughts for what they are and practice "threshold thinking." Take that first thought captive to the obedience of Christ. It is not a sin to be tempted, but entertaining those thoughts will lead to sin. If you consider them in your mind, your emotions will be stimulated in the wrong direction and your willpower will crumble. You should avoid any discussion with Satan's mouthpieces, which Eve failed to do when she answered, "God did say, 'You must not eat fruit from the tree that is in the middle of the garden, and you must not touch it, or you will die'" (3:3). Notice that she added the restriction, "you must not touch it." Don't continue to dialogue with the tempter—the person pushing you for sex or to have another piece of pie. "Let your 'Yes' be 'Yes,' and your 'No,' 'No,' lest you fall into judgment" (James 5:12 NKJV).

Satan had piqued her appetite for the forbidden fruit, and she saw "that the fruit of the tree was good for food" (verse 6). Her initial "no" was now a "maybe." It was through this same channel of temptation that the devil attempted to get Jesus to turn a rock into bread, which prompted Christ to quote Deuteronomy 8:3: "Man does not live on bread alone." There would have been nothing wrong with Jesus eating bread at the end of His fast, *except that it wasn't the Father's will for Him to do so.* He made His decision by verbally quoting Scripture, and that was the end of the dialogue. He was not about to act independently of the Father's will.

Eating is necessary and right, but eating too much—or eating the wrong kinds of foods, or allowing food to rule our lives—is wrong. Food sustains life, but it does not guarantee life, which is God's gift to those who trust in His Word and live by it. When we fast, we suppress the most powerful appetite we have, because food is necessary to sustain life. In a similar way, sex as intended by God is beautiful and good, but sex outside of marriage, fornication, and selfish sex are out of bounds and enslaving. If we give in to the temptation to meet our own fleshly desires independently of God, we are yielding to the lust of the flesh.

We all have residual flesh patterns that become points of vulnerability, and Satan seems to know just what buttons to push. What could be tempting to one person may not be at all tempting to another. It is important that we recognize our weaknesses and not subject ourselves to unnecessary temptation. We should also restrict our freedom for the sake of weaker Christians.

What is the key for believers in winning the battle for their minds?

_____

_____

_____

Why is it unwise to continue dialoguing with Satan's mouthpieces as Eve did in the Garden of Eden?

_____

_____

_____

_____

What is the difference between God's testing and the devil's tempting?

_____

_____

_____

_____

"One drink is too much" becomes "one drink is not enough" for those who give in to temptation. Can you identify the buttons that Satan is likely to push in your life?

_____

_____

_____

_____

How can "threshold thinking" become your way of escape?

_____

_____

_____

At this point James moves on from those external temptations which God sends to us for the testing of our faith to those internal ones which assault our souls and which are inspired by the devil. He wants to dispel the notion that the God who puts good thoughts into our minds also fills them with evil intentions. No one who has such wicked thoughts in his mind should ever try to claim that they come from God.

Bede (AD 673–735)

3

Lust of the Eyes

Deuteronomy 6:4–19

Key Point

Undermining God's Word destroys our confidence in Him.

Key Verses

My prayer is not that you take them out of the world but that you protect them from the evil one. . . . Sanctify them by the truth; your word is truth.

John 17:15, 17

Eve saw that the food was "pleasing to the eye" (Genesis 3:6). The "lust of the eyes" was the second channel of temptation through which Satan took advantage. Eve's resolve was weakening. *It looks good and I want it. What harm could possibly befall me if I took just one little bite?* Seizing the opportunity, Satan said, "You will not certainly die" (Genesis 3:4). "Don't listen to God," he hissed. "He is just trying to deny you some of life's great pleasures. Do what is right in your own eyes. There are no serious consequences for choices that you make."

The lust of the eyes subtly draws us away from the Word of God and eats away at our confidence in Him. We see what the world has to offer and desire it above our relationship with God. We begin to place more credence in our perspective of life than in God's plans and promises. Fueled by the lust for what we see, we grab for all that we can get. Tempting lies have not changed since the original sin. *Go ahead and do it. You know you want to. Everyone else is doing it. Why should you be denied? Who would know if you did? You will get away with it.*

With Eve, Satan questioned the Word of God. With Jesus, he quoted Scripture, but in a diabolical way. "If you believe God's Word is true, prove it. Jump off the Temple wall. God will save you by sending His angels to bear you up. You won't even come close to hitting the rocks below" (paraphrase of Matthew 4:6). Had Jesus jumped to His death, everyone's confidence in God would have been shattered.

However, Jesus was not going to be seduced by a passage taken out of context. He countered the temptation with a passage of Scripture that exposed Satan's ploy: "Do not put the Lord your God to the test" (Deuteronomy 6:16). That verse follows the Shema (see Deuteronomy 6:4–9), which is still recited daily by orthodox Jews. Shema means "to hear so as to obey."

The righteous live by faith in the written Word of God and do not demand that God prove Himself in response to our whims or wishes, no matter how noble we think our cause may be. God is under no obligation to us—He is under obligation only to Himself. There is no way that we can cleverly word a prayer so that God must respond to our will. Such thinking distorts the meaning of prayer and puts us in the position of trying to manipulate God.

A beloved man was once dying with cancer. Word spread throughout his church that four independent witnesses had all testified that the man was not going to die. The congregation believed these witnesses had heard from God and rejoiced. Three weeks later, the man died. Either those four "witnesses" were paying attention to a deceiving spirit, or God's Word can't be trusted.

Counterfeit gifts of knowledge and prophecy spoken through false prophets and deceived Christians can destroy our confidence in God. If they give us a "word from the Lord" and it doesn't prove to be true, God can no longer be trusted. The same thing happens if we pay attention to a deceiving spirit and think it is from God. Paul says that we will fall away from the faith if we pay attention to deceiving spirits and things taught by demons (see 1 Timothy 4:1).

How will people behave if they believe there are no negative long-term or short-term consequences for their choices?

_____

_____

_____

How can false prophecies and deceiving spirits undermine our confidence in God?

_____

_____

_____

Are there ways that we can pray and use Scripture in such a way that God is obligated to respond favorably to us?

_____

_____

_____

Have you ever wanted something that looks good and wondered why God wouldn't want you to have it? How is rationalizing a sinful decision questioning God's Word?

_____

_____

_____

Do you believe that universalism, the belief that all will be saved, questions God's Word?

_____

_____

_____

What can the reason be that with each temptation the devil adds, "If you are the Son of God"? He is acting just like he did in the case of Adam, when he disparaged God by saying, "In the day you eat, your eyes will be opened." So he does in this case, intending thereby to signify that our first parents had been beguiled and outsmarted and had received no benefit. So even in the temptation of Jesus he insinuates the same thing, saying, "In vain God has called you 'Son' and has beguiled you by his gift. For, if this is not so, give us some clear proof that you are from that power."

John Chrysostom (AD 347–407)

4

The Pride of Life

Proverbs 16:16–24

Key Point

A proud Christian benefits Satan more than an atheist or pagan.

Key Verse

Pride goes before destruction, a haughty spirit before a fall.

Proverbs 16:18

Eve saw that the tree was "desirable for gaining wisdom" (Genesis 3:6). The chink in her armor was now a gaping hole, and Satan drove the final stake: "God knows that when you eat from it your eyes will be opened, and you will be like God, knowing good and evil" (verse 5). Eve's resolve finally crumpled under the pride of life, and "she took some and ate it."

Satan's promise that the couple would become like God was a lie he knew well, as he had believed it once himself. His own pride precipitated his fall from heaven. His objective was to get Adam and Eve to lose their dominion, and when that happened he filled the vacant post and became the prince of this world. Satan tried the same ploy with Jesus when he offered Him the kingdoms of this world if He would bow down and worship him. In other words, "I'll pay you to praise me." Such incredible vainglory. Jesus commanded Satan to leave, declaring that He would worship and serve God only (see Matthew 4:10).

By appealing to the pride of life, Satan intends to steer us away from the worship of God and destroy our obedience to Him. Whenever we think that we don't need God's help or direction—that we can handle our lives without consulting Him and that we don't have to bow our knee to anyone—we must be prepared for a fall. When we stop worshiping and serving God, we are serving the god of this world, and that is what he wants more than anything else.

Satan and pride are intricately connected. "God opposes the proud but shows favor to the humble. Submit yourselves, then, to God. Resist the devil, and he will flee from you" (James 4:6–7). "Humble yourselves, therefore, under God's mighty hand, that he may lift you up in due time. . . . Your enemy the devil prowls around like a roaring lion looking for someone to devour" (1 Peter 5:6, 8).

From our earliest years we crave for attention. Little boys show off and little girls wear padded bras and paint their faces. Actors and musicians keep adding award shows. A football player makes a great tackle and draws attention to himself. *Hey, look at me!* Christians have their own award shows and build their own monuments. A proud Christian benefits Satan more than an atheist or pagan. A lot more would be accomplished in the kingdom of God if we didn't care who received the credit.

Remember that there are three critical issues reflected in the channels of temptation. First, the lust of the flesh will draw us away from the will of God and destroy our dependence on Him. Second, the lust of the eyes will draw us away from the Word of God and destroy our confidence in Him. Third, the boastful pride of life will draw us away from our worship of God and destroy our humble obedience to Him.

The temptation to have power and influence apart from God has destroyed many ministries. We have to build God's kingdom, not ours. We have to glorify the Lord and not seek glory for ourselves. We have to find our worth in our relationship with God and not in human accomplishments. When we do, the King of kings and the Lord of lords will bless us.

What lie did Satan know well? What did it cost him? What did it cost Eve?

_____

_____

_____

How much was Satan willing to give up just to gain acknowledgment? What are people giving up to gain the same?

_____

_____

_____

Why are people in such desperate need for attention? What are they lacking?

_____

_____

_____

How do you feel when someone gets more attention than you do or gets more credit than you do for the same accomplishment? How does that leave you feeling vulnerable?

_____

_____

_____

_____

Do you find it hard to give God all the glory? Why? Do you believe that God wants to exult you? How could that happen?

_____

_____

_____

The stronger you are in your faith, the greater will be your confidence that you can overcome the wiles of the devil. You will also be aided in this endeavor by the knowledge that what you are going through is something common to the fellowship of all Christians throughout the world. Ever since the beginning of time it has been the lot of the righteous to suffer, and what a shame it would be if you were to be the only ones unable to endure this.

Bede (AD 673–735)

5

Too Much of a Good Thing

1 Corinthians 6:12–20

Key Point

Do all things in moderation.

Key Verses

The LORD is my shepherd, I shall not want. He makes me lie down in green pastures; He leads me beside quiet waters. He restores my soul; He guides me in the paths of righteousness for His name's sake.

Psalm 23:1–3 NASB

Satan is too clever and subtle to tempt committed Christians to do perverse and grossly immoral deeds. He knows that they will recognize the flagrant wrong in such temptations and refuse to act on them. His tactic is to push something good beyond the will of God until it becomes sin. He treats us like the proverbial frog in the pot of water, gradually turning up the heat of temptation in the hopes that we won't notice that we are approaching the boundary of God's will and jump out before it becomes sin.

"If you find honey, eat just enough—too much of it, and you will vomit" (Proverbs 25:16). In other words, do all things in moderation. Paul writes, "'I have the right to do anything' . . . but not everything is beneficial. 'I have the right to do anything'—but I will not be mastered by anything" (1 Corinthians 6:12). Paul sees nothing but green lights in every direction of the Christian life. Everything is good and lawful for us because we are free from sin and no longer under the condemnation of the law. However, Paul also knows that if we irresponsibly floorboard our lives in any of these good and lawful directions, we will eventually run the red lights of God's will. Having a glass of wine with your meal is fine, but drinking the whole bottle isn't.

It is possible to have too much of a good thing. Physical rest becomes laziness. Quietness becomes noncommunication. The ability to profit becomes avarice or greed. The enjoyment of life becomes intemperance. Physical pleasure becomes sensuality. Interest in the possessions of others becomes covetousness. Enjoyment of food becomes gluttony. Self-care becomes selfishness. Self-respect becomes conceit. Communication becomes gossip. Cautiousness becomes insensitivity. Anger becomes a bad temper and rage. Lovingkindness becomes overprotection. Judgment becomes criticism. Same-sex friendships become homosexuality. Sexual freedom becomes immorality. Conscientiousness becomes perfectionism. Generosity becomes wastefulness. Self-protection becomes dishonesty. Carefulness becomes fear.

If the devil can't make you immoral, he will drive you to extremes. One time, a pastor was surprised when the wife of his associate asked for a personal appointment. She was the hardest worker in the church. What the pastor didn't know was that she was also the most driven person in the church. Keeping busy was her way of keeping her sanity. Such is the case with many workaholics; they can't tolerate solitude.

The devil drives you. God leads you. One person who went through the Steps said it well: "I have discovered a feeling of control—like my mind is my own. I haven't had these strung-out periods of thought and contemplations—i.e., conversations with myself. My mind just feels quieted. My emotions have been stable, and I haven't felt depressed once this week. My will is mine, and I feel left alone. Not in a bad way—I'm not lonely, just a single person. I feel capable of helping people and of handling myself. I've been co-dependent for years, but this last week I haven't had the slightest need for someone. I am at peace and feel this quiet, soft joy in my heart. Thank you for lending me your hope. I believe I have my own now in Christ."

What is a Christian free to do? What does freedom look like?

_____

_____

_____

_____

What did Paul mean in 1 Corinthians 6:12 when he said, "I have the right to do anything . . . but not everything is beneficial"?

_____

_____

_____

What is the difference between being called and being driven?

_____

_____

_____

What excesses have caused you problems in the past?

_____

_____

_____

How can you set boundaries for yourself?

_____

_____

_____

Paul means that if we are free to choose, then we should remain free and not become a slave to any particular desire. Anyone who orders his desires properly remains the master of them, but once he goes beyond the limit he loses control and becomes their slave.

John Chrysostom (AD 347–407)

Overcoming Accusation

It seemed to be his lot. He was one of those unfortunate people with a talent to be always in the wrong place, always at the wrong time. He was born wrong—the declining Roman empire, the broken home, the conquered Jewish nation, the poverty stricken slums. He lived wrong. Others went to school. He played hooky. Others played ball. He stole apples. Others learned trades. He learned to cheat. Just a common thief. He started wrong. He lived wrong, and it looked as if he'd finish wrong—the wrong place and the wrong time—a Roman cross, a painful death, a final shame.

When from the middle cross came words of redeeming love, "You shall be with me in paradise." In all the stream of history one and only one of the numberless sons of Adam could have said those words, and he hung beside him. What tremendous fortune—what wondrous providence. In one instant his life—given to evil, thoroughly misused, doomed to die—was changed and ended in crowning glory. It was one sentence without which there is no success. It was the one sentence which redeems all failure, and it was said to him at life's final flickering moment. The one most important issue of all was gloriously solved. At long last he was in the right place at the right time![1]

—Bob Benson, *Laughter in the Walls*

Daily Readings

1. The Accuser	Zechariah 3:1–10
2. Jesus Our Advocate	Hebrews 7:23–28
3. The Narrow Way	Matthew 7:13–23
4. The Unpardonable Sin	Mark 3:22–30
5. Betrayal and Restoration	John 21:15–19

1

The Accuser

Zechariah 3:1–10

Key Point

Satan has no basis for accusing those who are clothed in Christ's righteousness.

Key Verse

When they hurled their insults at him, he did not retaliate; when he suffered, he made no threats. Instead, he entrusted himself to him who judges justly.

1 Peter 2:23

The Lord revealed to Zechariah a heavenly scene in which Satan's accusations of God's people were put in perspective (see Zechariah 3:1–10). The cast of characters resembled a heavenly courtroom. God the Father was the judge. Satan was the prosecuting attorney. Joshua, the high priest who represented all of God's people, was the accused.

Under the Law, the high priest would enter the Holy of Holies once a year on the great Day of Atonement. It was an awesome experience to go before a manifestation of a Holy God. The high priest would go through elaborate purification rites so that he could enter God's presence ceremonially undefiled. Over time, it became the practice to tie bells around the hem of his garment and ropes around his legs. The other priests would stay outside the veil and listen for the bells, and if they heard no movement, they would use the rope to pull the priest out, as no one else dared to enter.

Now Joshua was standing before God in filthy clothes. Not a good thing! However, "the Lord said to Satan, 'The Lord rebuke you, Satan! The Lord, who has chosen Jerusalem, rebuke you! Is not this man a burning stick snatched from the fire?'" (verse 2). God rebuked the devil, not Joshua. "For the accuser of our brothers and sisters, who accuses them before our God day and night, has been hurled down" (Revelation 12:10). What the devil didn't count on was Jesus being our defense attorney. Because of Christ's work on the cross, there is no way we are going to lose this court case. Every born-again child of God has been snatched from the fires of hell.

Satan is not the judge. He cannot decide a verdict or pronounce a sentence. He can only bring accusations. The reason Satan's accusations are groundless is because God has solved the problem of our filthy garments. He has removed them and clothed us in Christ's righteousness. While Satan is bringing charges against us in heaven, his emissaries also accuse us personally by bombarding our minds with false thoughts about our unworthiness and unrighteousness. *How could you do that and be a Christian? You're not really a child of God. God doesn't love you, and He isn't going to save you.* If that doesn't work, his evil spirits pepper us with blasphemous or foul thoughts that we think are our own, which causes us to question our salvation.

Freedom in Christ Ministries once contracted with George Barna to conduct a survey of people in the Church. The participants were given a set of statements to which they could respond, "strongly agree," "somewhat agree," "somewhat disagree," "strongly disagree," or "don't know." Fifty-seven percent strongly agreed and 25 percent somewhat agreed with the statement "The Christian life is well summed-up as 'trying hard to do what God commands.'" Fifty-eight percent strongly or somewhat agreed with the statement "I feel like I don't measure up to God's expectations of me.[1] Apparently, legalism is still plaguing many believers. How could you not feel condemned if you are living under the Law? "Such regulations indeed have an appearance of wisdom, with their self-imposed worship, their false humility, and their harsh treatment of the body, but they lack any value in restraining sensual indulgence" (Colossians 2:23).

Who were in the cast of characters in Zechariah's vision?

In the vision, Joshua, the high priest, wore filthy clothes in violation of the Temple purification laws. Yet why did God not rebuke him?

Given that the Church has been under the grace of God for 2,000 years, why do you think so many people struggle with legalism?

Would you agree or disagree with the research statements cited in this reading?

Legalists don't know they are legalists; they see themselves as defenders of the faith. How, then, can people know whether or not legalism is a problem for them?

Because of his accusations and calumny against people, he has been called "accuser," which he is. The angels rejoice at his downfall, for faith has nothing to do with faithlessness. And although the saints have been accused and slandered by him, as was also Job, yet by their suffering for the sake of Christ they have conquered him as well as all those who trusted in Him.

Andrew of Caesarea (AD 563–637)

2

Jesus Our Advocate

Hebrews 7:23–28

Key Point

Jesus died once for all our sin and now is our advocate before our heavenly Father.

Key Verse

Who will bring any charge against those whom God has chosen?

Romans 8:33

The book of Hebrews starts by presenting Jesus as greater than the angels, greater than Moses, and all other mortals. The purpose of Hebrews is to help the Church transition from the Old Covenant of law to the New Covenant of grace. Under the Mosaic Law, the priests would continue offering sacrifices for sins. That is no longer necessary, because Jesus died once for all our sins (see Hebrews 7:23–24, Romans 6:6–10).

What is Jesus doing now? "My dear children, I write this to you so that you will not sin. But if anybody does sin, we have an advocate with the Father—Jesus Christ, the Righteous One" (1 John 2:1). What follows is the testimony of someone who transitioned from the Old to the New Covenant.

> For as long as I can remember I have struggled with extremely low self-esteem and a crippling lack of confidence. I remember writing several times in my diary when I was fifteen, "I hate myself. Why can't I be like . . . [anyone other than myself]?" I had a bleak outlook on my future and just figured I would never change. This entire time I was a born-again Christian and knew Christ had saved me at age seven. I was raised in a Bible-believing Christian home and church.
>
> When going through the Steps to Freedom in Christ, I finally stepped back and saw that one of the major root causes of my horrible sense of embarrassment, crippling regret, and shame was the legalistic form of Christianity in which I was raised. The difficult thing about legalism is that grace can appear to be preached, but what is acted out is judgmental, critical, perfectionistic, and performance-based living. Finally, I began to understand that my relationship with God was not based on how early I got up in the morning to pray, or how well I knew my Bible, or how sin-free I managed to keep myself, or how committed I was to church activities.
>
> I had grown up with no comprehension of how to feel accepted by God just as I was, without having to first fulfill an impossible list of requirements. The whole thing was one big guilt trip. I was racked by guilt for not being able to pray the way I knew I should, for not feeling like God was hearing me, and for not enjoying reading the Bible. I felt obliged to be at every service, and I eagerly wanted people to think of me as holy, spiritually minded, and a strong Christian, even though I wasn't any of those things.
>
> The teaching I had received as a teen convinced me that God had abandoned me because of my struggle with particular sins. The verse "If I had cherished sin in my heart, the Lord would not have listened" (Psalm 66:18) rang in my ears every time I tried to pray. That left me in limbo-land: unable to pray and unable to stop sinning. Everyone was keeping up the pretense of perfection and holiness. No one let on that they were struggling with sin, or experiencing any lack of closeness to God.

This woman was a testimony to what Paul wrote in Galatians 3:10: "All who rely on the works of the law are under a curse." Thankfully, she became a living testimony that "Christ redeemed us from the curse of the law by becoming a curse for us" (verse 13).

Why does Jesus need to speak to the Father in our defense?

_____

_____

_____

What happens to people in a congregation where grace is taught but not lived?

_____

_____

_____

How can we create an atmosphere in our churches and small groups where people feel free to share with one another?

_____

_____

_____

To which parts of the lady's testimony in this reading do you most relate? Do you think her story is an isolated case or a common one? Explain.

_____

_____

_____

_____

Grace is a balance between legalism and license. What steps do you need to make to stay balanced?

_____

_____

_____

I will not glory because I have been redeemed. I will not glory because I am free of sins, but because sins have been forgiven me. I will not glory because I am profitable or because anyone is profitable to me, but because Christ is my advocate on my behalf before the Father, because the blood of Christ has been poured out on my behalf.

Ambrose (AD 340–397)

3

The Narrow Way
Matthew 7:13–23

Key Point

Satan only accuses those who take the narrow way.

Key Verses

Enter through the narrow gate. For wide is the gate and broad is the road that leads to destruction, and many enter through it. But small is the gate and narrow the road that leads to life, and only a few find it.

Matthew 7:13–14

The grace walk is like a narrow mountain road that is always climbing upward. On one side of the road is a cliff. It is too high to jump off and too steep to climb down. On the other side is a roaring forest fire. There is a roaring lion looking for an opportunity to divert you off the path. Christ is setting the pace just ahead of you, urging you not to look either to the left or the right.

If you take your eyes off Jesus, you will be tempted to consider the first option. You will throw off the restraints and just sail off that cliff. It would be wise to consider the sudden stop at the end. Having no restraints may appear like freedom, but license only leads to destruction.

The other option is the roaring fire of legalism with flames of condemnation. Even the broad way has civil laws, or they would have social chaos—and people generally accept that. When someone goes five miles faster than the speed limit, he or she doesn't think, *Oh woe is me; I'm a terrible person.* All the restraints are external, and the fear of paying the fine keeps them in check. Satan's only role for pagans is to keep them blinded.

Christians have the law within them. The Holy Spirit will convict us of sin, which leads to repentance without regret. There is no condemnation for those who are in Christ Jesus (see Romans 8:1). "Perfect love drives out fear, because fear has to do with punishment" (1 John 4:18). Churches that are bound in legalism are just helping the devil bring accusations against believers. God intended local churches to be a place where people got rid of the guilt, not have it piled on.

The tempter will whisper, "Go ahead and do it. You know you want it. Everybody is doing it, and you will get away with it." If we give in to the tempter, he will immediately change roles and become the accuser: "How can you call yourself a Christian and do *that*? You will never get away with it."

The struggle in our minds is like walking through a narrow door and seeing Jesus ahead of us. Lining the narrow street are buildings with people popping their heads out of doors and windows to tempt us and accuse us. "You don't believe this religious garbage, do you? Come on in with the rest of us and have a good time." The most defeated Christians pay attention to those deceptive lies. They sit down in defeat and make no progress toward Christ.

The second-most defeated Christians appear to be fighting the good fight. They combat every fiery dart. "No, you're not going to entice me. That's not true. You can't accuse me." Yet they are allowing the devil to set the agenda. They end up standing in the street and making little progress toward Christ.

Victorious Christians put up the shield of faith, fix their eyes on Jesus, and keep walking by faith in the power of the Holy Spirit. They don't pay attention to deceiving spirits. At first the battle for their mind is intense, but as they continue walking by faith the narrow path gets broader and broader. The mental assault gets less and less intense as they draw closer to Christ.

Why do so many people fail to consider the long-term consequences of their decisions?

_____

_____

_____

Why do we feel so less condemned by breaking civil laws?

_____

_____

_____

If God isn't accusing or condemning us, who is? How do we know?

_____

_____

_____

Why do you think so many Christians feel condemned and defeated?

_____

_____

_____

Why do you feel less condemned when you transgress a civil law than a moral law? Aren't both moral? Explain.

_____

_____

_____

Remember that later Jesus would say, "My yoke is easy, and burden light." And here He implies the same thing [Matthew 7:13]. Does it seem inconsistent then to say here that the good road is narrow and constricted? Pay attention. He has made it clear the burden is very light, easy, and agreeable. "But how," one may say, "is the narrow and constricted road easy?" Because it is both a gate and a road. The other road is, of course, both a gate and a road, but on that way there is nothing that is enduring. All things on that way are temporary, both things pleasant and painful.

John Chrysostom (AD 347–407)

4

The Unpardonable Sin

Mark 3:22–30

Key Point

Christians cannot commit the unpardonable sin because they are already pardoned.

Key Verse

So we see that they were not able to enter, because of their unbelief.

Hebrews 3:19

In Mark 3:22–30, teachers of the Law came from Jerusalem to accuse Jesus of being possessed by Beelzebul, whose name means "lord of the flies." The teachers thought Jesus was driving out demons through the power of this prince of demons who dwelt within Him. Jesus answered this absurd charge by saying, "How can Satan drive out Satan? If a kingdom is divided against itself, that kingdom cannot stand. If a house is divided against itself, that house cannot stand. And if Satan opposes himself and is divided, he cannot stand; his end has come" (verses 23–26). Obviously, Satan's kingdom of darkness continues to function.

Jesus then gave an argument related to the strong man's house. Satan is the strong man, and his house is the realm of sin, sickness, and death. His possessions are the people he holds captive to do his will. No one can enter his realm and plunder his possessions unless they first bind the strong man—in other words, have greater power and authority. Jesus can bind the strong man, rob the realm, and release the captives. Jesus demonstrated His superiority over Satan when He was tempted and by His ability to cast out demons.

Many believers struggle with the false belief that they have committed the unpardonable sin by blaspheming the Holy Spirit. Those who are tormented by this fear usually suffer in silence. Jesus said, "People can be forgiven all their sins and every slander they utter, but whoever blasphemes against the Holy Spirit will never be forgiven; they are guilty of an eternal sin" (Mark 3:28–29). Matthew adds to this statement: "Anyone who speaks a word against the Son of Man will be forgiven, but anyone who speaks against the Holy Spirit will not be forgiven, either in this age or in the age to come" (Matthew 12:32).

Why can we blaspheme one member of the Trinity and not another? It has to do with the unique works of Christ and the Holy Spirit. The work of the Holy Spirit is to draw all people to Christ. If you reject that witness, then you will never come to Christ and experience salvation. The work of Christ is to forgive all who come to Him by faith. Those who do come to Christ are children of God, and their sins and blasphemies are forgiven because they are in Christ. If you reject the witness of God's Spirit, then you never come to Christ in the first place.

This is why Christians cannot commit the unpardonable sin—because they are already pardoned. The only unpardonable sin is the sin of unbelief. The Jewish leaders were committing the unpardonable sin by ascribing the spiritual power of Christ to Beelzebul. Christians who question the work of the Holy Spirit in people or ministries are not committing the unpardonable sin. They may be wisely testing the spirit, or wrongly quenching or grieving the Spirit, but neither of these is unpardonable.

An eighty-one-year-old retired missionary widow invested her life in reaching female prisoners in the city of Manila in the Philippines. She had a burden for training Christian prisoners to evangelize and lead other prisoners through the Steps to Freedom in Christ. They have been successful with mental patients, restoring them from a life of being inactive in their beds to having Christ as their personal savior. Read her story of binding the strong man on the following page.

How did Jesus respond to the charges that He was driving out demons through the power of Beelzebul?

_____

_____

_____

What did Jesus mean when He said that "no one can enter a strong man's house without first tying him up"?

_____

_____

_____

Why is it unpardonable to blaspheme the work of the Holy Spirit?

_____

_____

_____

How would you help those who think they have committed the unpardonable sin?

_____

_____

_____

How do you think sincere believers would feel if they thought they had committed the unpardonable sin?

_____

_____

_____

The adversary enticed humanity to transgress our Maker's law, and thereby got us into his clutches. Yet his power consisted only in tempting the human will toward trespasses and apostasy. With these chains he bound up the human will. This is why in the economy of salvation it was necessary that he be bound with the same chains by which he bound humanity. It would be through a man that humanity would be set free to return to the Lord, leaving the adversary in those bonds by which he himself had been fettered; that is, sin. For when Satan is bound, man is set free, since "none can enter a strong man's house and spoil his goods, unless he first bind the strong man himself."

Irenaeus (AD 130–202)

Setting Captives Free

After I retired from being a missionary, I found I had a burden for seeing prisoners in the Manila, Philippines, Correctional Institution for Women come to Christ and help their fellow prisoners find Christ. In this endeavor I was joined by Filipina, an experienced Christian leader who started fifteen churches during her thirty-five years of ministry. However, Filipina and I recently tackled a person who was way beyond our experience.

Her name was Naomi. She was more than forty years old at the time and had been the terror of the prison, beating people up at will. Even the administration feared her. Naomi had four demon "helpers" who aided her in doing anything she wished. They even blurred the vision of jail guards so that she could walk out of the prison with no one stopping her. It was a year before she returned to prison. During that time, she supposedly murdered seven people.

Unaware of her background, Filipina and I shared the gospel with her and led her to Christ. She professed salvation at our Bible study and was eager to change, but our trainees had been cruelly persecuted by her for as many as ten years and did not trust her sincerity. Naomi revealed that when she was ten years old, her witch doctor grandfather implanted some amulets in her and apparently gave her his psychic legacy. She requested our help to free her from demons, so we took her through the Steps to Freedom in Christ.

Naomi writhed in pain during the process but stuck with it, even though she had severe abdominal pain and could not eat or drink for four days. Finally, the amulets planted by her grandfather were expelled, and her demon assistants appeared to leave. She experienced breakthrough after fasting and praying when she begged the Lord to reveal why the devil was not allowing her to eat and drink. The Lord reminded her of the magic books, amulets, dolls, and other paraphernalia she possessed. She thought about burning them, but fires are not allowed in the prison. So she loaded them in a travel bag and delivered them to the garbage truck.

Naomi was now totally free and a bold witness for the Lord. Then a miracle happened. She was called to the Justice Department and told that the judges had selected her for release within four months. We have had a spirit of revival, with souls being saved every week. "The Spirit of the Lord is on me, because he has anointed me to proclaim good news to the poor. He has sent me to proclaim freedom for the prisoners and recovery of sight for the blind, to set the oppressed free, to proclaim the year of the Lord's favor" (Luke 4:18–19).

5

Betrayal and Restoration

John 21:15–19

Key Point

The conviction of the Holy Spirit leads to restoration with Christ.

Key Verse

For we are God's handiwork, created in Christ Jesus to do good works, which God prepared in advance for us to do.

Ephesians 2:10

Many Christians struggle with a deep-seated sense of self-deprecation. They don't feel important, qualified, or good for anything. They are paralyzed in their witness and productivity by their thoughts and feelings of inferiority and worthlessness. Satan's lies and accusations have left them questioning their salvation and God's love. They were created "in Christ Jesus to do good works," which is being inhibited by the accuser. In truth they are unconditionally loved and accepted by Him. God's love (*agape*) and acceptance is unconditional, because His love is based on who He is and not on who we are or how well we behave.

Peter was struggling with condemning thoughts and feelings of worthlessness because he had betrayed Christ three times. His work, which God had prepared for him, was over. He had failed. So he went back to fishing, but he caught nothing. Then a stranger on the shore said, "Throw your net on the right side of the boat and you will find some" (John 21:6). After they caught 153 fish, they suddenly recognized it was Jesus. When they came ashore, Jesus had a fire going for them and said, "Come and have breakfast" (verse 12). Amazing grace! That was the third time Jesus had appeared to them.

"When they had finished eating, Jesus said to Simon Peter, 'Simon son of John, do you love [*agape*] me more than these?' 'Yes, Lord,' he said, 'you know that I love [*phileo*] you'" (verses 15–16). *Phileo* is brotherly love, which is more like a natural affection. However, that was good enough, because soon the love *(agape)* of God would be within Peter. Jesus was saying, "If you really love Me, get out of the boat, back into ministry, and shepherd the flock. I didn't call you to be a fisherman but a fisher of men."

You can stumble and fall and remain on the ground listening to the accuser, or you can get back up and listen to God. He is saying, "I knew you from the foundation of this world. I have forgiven you and created you in Christ for good works. I will be with you to the ends of the earth, and I will never leave you or forsake you." Settle it now, once and for all time.

Read the following declaration and verbally express it if you agree: "I believe in my heart that Jesus died for my sins and that God raised Him from the dead in order that I may have eternal life. I confess with my mouth that Jesus is Lord. I renounce any efforts on my part to save myself. I choose to believe that I am saved by the grace of God through faith and that I am now a child of God because of His great mercy. I believe that God has transferred me out of the kingdom of darkness and into the kingdom of His beloved Son. I renounce the lies and accusations of Satan that would rob me of my full assurance of eternal life. I choose to take every thought captive and make it obedient to Christ. I put on the helmet of salvation and lift up the shield of faith against Satan's fiery darts. I submit myself to God and ask Him to fill me with His Holy Spirit. In the name of the Lord Jesus Christ, I command Satan and all his evil spirits to depart from me. I belong to God for all eternity."

Why do so many Christians drop out of ministry?

Is there any significance to knowing that Jesus used the word *phileo* when He asked the third time, "Simon son of John, do you love me" (verse 17)?

How effective is the accuser of the brethren?

How do you feel after experiencing a disappointment in ministry?

What do you do after you stumble and fall? What should you do?

What benefit could Peter confer on Christ by the mere fact of his loving Christ? If Christ loves you, it is to your advantage, not Christ's. And if you love Christ, it is to your advantage, not Christ's. And yet Christ the Lord wanted to indicate how people ought to show that they love Christ. And He made it plain enough by entrusting him with his sheep. "Do you love Me?" "I do." "Feed my sheep." Peter made no other reply than that he loved Him. The Lord asked no other question, but whether he loved Him. When Peter answered, our Lord did nothing else but entrust His sheep to him.

Augustine of Hippo (AD 354–430)

Overcoming Deception

The Catechism of the Catholic Church states, "The Church is apostolic because she is founded on the apostles, in three ways: (1) she was and remains built on 'the foundation of the Apostles, the witnesses chosen and sent on mission by Christ himself;' (2) with the help of the Spirit dwelling in her, the Church keeps and hands on the teaching, the 'good deposit,' the salutary words she has heard from the apostles; (3) she continues to be taught, sanctified and guided by the apostles until Christ's return, through their successors in pastoral office."[1]

The Orthodox Church holds to the same apostolic succession but doesn't acknowledge the pope as the supreme (singular) pastor. The Church has not historically taught that there would be more apostles than the ones selected by Christ during His earthly ministry and, later, the apostle Paul. That is the position held by the Reformers and most evangelical churches today.

Why, then, are some Christians around the world identifying their leaders as "apostles" and "prophets"? Some are even self-appointed. Have the titles of apostle and prophet taken on a new meaning? Is the whole Church supposed to accept what these apostles and prophets say as authoritative in the same way we understand Scripture? Are they good people who just have the wrong title? Are some trying to enhance their status, or are they false apostles, prophets, and teachers that Scripture warns us about?

Daily Readings

1. Confronting Deception	James 1:13–25
2. False Prophets and Teachers	Jeremiah 23:14–32
3. Signs and Wonders	Deuteronomy 13:1–18
4. Counterfeits Within the Church	2 Peter 2:1–10
5. Testing the Spirits	1 John 3:21–4:6

1

Confronting Deception
James 1:13–25

Key Point

If you are deceived, you don't know it.

Key Verse

An honest witness does not deceive, but a false witness pours out lies.

Proverbs 14:5

Satan tempts us to sin and stops us in our tracks by accusations, but his most insidious weapon is deception, because we don't know when we are being deceived. Through deception, the father of lies has led the whole world astray (see Revelation 12:9). That is why truth sets us free and why the belt of truth is the first piece of our protective armor. Jesus prayed that we would be kept from the evil one by being sanctified in the truth of God's Word (see John 17:15–17). James admonished us not to be deceived (see James 1:16). There are three primary avenues through which we can be deceived: (1) self-deception, (2) false prophets/teachers, and (3) deceiving spirits. Scripture identifies at least eight ways that we can deceive ourselves.

First, *we can deceive ourselves if we listen to the Word of God but don't do it* (see James 1:22–25). "All Scripture is God-breathed and is useful for teaching, rebuking, correcting and training in righteousness" (2 Timothy 3:16). We will be self-deceived if we think the Bible is just a textbook that provides us with knowledge. We will hardly be aware of how self-centered and self-righteous we are, but others will likely see the hypocrisy. When the Bible is a mirror, it knocks us down a notch, picks us back up, and trains us in righteousness.

Second, *we can deceive ourselves if we say we have no sin* (see 1 John 1:8). Having sin and being sin are two different issues. We are not sinless saints; we are saints who sin. If we keep saying that we have done nothing wrong, we may start believing it.

Third, *we can deceive ourselves if we think we are something when we are not* (see Romans 12:3; Galatians 6:3). We are children of God, by the grace of God, who are living our lives before God. Those who think they are special don't know they really are!

Fourth, *we can deceive ourselves when we think we are wise in this age* (see 1 Corinthians 3:18–19). In professing ourselves to be wise we become fools (see Romans 1:22). "The foolishness of God is wiser than human wisdom" (1 Corinthians 1:25). Wisdom is seeing life from God's perspective, not ours. Someday, we shall see fully, but right now we have one eye starting to slightly open. We don't have a clue what is going on right around us in the spiritual realm.

Fifth, *we can deceive ourselves when we think we are religious but do not keep a tight rein on our tongue* (see James 1:26). Spirit-filled Christians exhibit self-control and only use their words to build up others (see Ephesians 4:29–30). Those who can't control their tongues are denying the anger within them.

Sixth, *we can deceive ourselves when we think we will not reap what we sow* (see Galatians 6:7). Everything we think and do has consequences, and we will one day give an account for our words and our actions.

Seventh, *we can deceive ourselves when we think the unrighteous will inherit the kingdom of God* (see 1 Corinthians 6:9–10). We cannot defend a sinful lifestyle and claim to be Christians by calling sin something other than what it is.

Eighth, *we can deceive ourselves when we associate with bad company and think it will not corrupt us* (see 1 Corinthians 15:33). Sin is contagious. "Therefore let him who thinks he stands take heed that he does not fall" (1 Corinthians 10:12 NASB).

Why is it so hard to help someone who is self-deceived?

_____

_____

_____

How many of the eight self-deceptions listed above are related to pride? How could they be avoided if we humbled ourselves?

_____

_____

_____

How can people not know that they will reap what they sow and won't be contaminated by bad company?

_____

_____

_____

Think of some people you know who are living a lie but don't know it. Should you help them? How?

_____

_____

_____

To which of the above eight means of self-deception are you most susceptible? Why?

_____

_____

_____

*Do not deceive yourselves by coming eagerly to hear the Word
and then failing to do it. If it is a good thing to hear, it is a
much better thing to do. If you do not hear, you cannot do,
and therefore you will build nothing. But if you hear and do
not do, then what you are building will be ruin.*

Augustine of Hippo (AD 354–430)

2

False Prophets and Teachers
Jeremiah 23:14–32

Key Point

True prophets draw people back to God and His Word.

Key Verses

For there is one God and one mediator between God and mankind, the man Christ Jesus, who gave himself as a ransom for all people. This has now been witnessed to at the proper time.

1 Timothy 2:5–6

Every true prophet of God in the Old Testament was similar to a New Testament evangelist. The genuine prophet drew people back to God and His Word, and this call to righteous living separated him from the false prophet. Through the prophet Jeremiah, God warned His people not to pay attention to false prophets who were speaking words of encouragement to those who despised God (see Jeremiah 23:16–17). God said His prophets would proclaim His words to His people and turn them from their evil ways and their evil deeds (see verse 22).

Those who prophesied lies in God's name were professing to have received their messages from dreams, but their messages were delusions from their own minds. "'Let the prophet who has a dream recount the dream, but let the one who has my word speak it faithfully. For what has straw to do with grain?' declares the LORD" (verse 28). God had spoken through dreams, but the false prophets' dreams were like straw that had no nutritional value at all compared to the grain of God's Word.

Straw is good for bedding livestock, but livestock will die if that is all they are fed. We get our spiritual nutrition from God's Word. If a prophetic message were to come to your church, it wouldn't be comforting to those church members who were living in sin. His Word is "like a hammer that breaks a rock in pieces" (verse 29). The Spirit of God is not going to lull His people into a spirit of complacency, because judgment begins in the household of God (see 1 Peter 4:17). A prophetic message should motivate people to live righteous lives, not placate them in their sin (see 1 Corinthians 14:24–25).

God is also against those prophets who steal His words from others (see Jeremiah 23:30). It is plagiarism to take what God has given someone else and use it as though it were your own. God is also against "the prophets who wag their own tongues and yet declare, 'The LORD declares'" (verse 31). Saying that your words are directly from the Lord when they aren't is an offense to God. Manipulating people by claiming a word from the Lord is spiritual abuse. For a man to tell a young lady that God has told him they are supposed to get married is incredibly manipulative. If she wrongly thinks he is a man of God, then to refuse marriage is to refuse God. If God wanted them to get married, why wouldn't He tell both of them?

False prophets may also try to guide our lives by giving us specific instructions for daily living and decision-making. "God told me that you are supposed to do so and so," they say. False prophets usurp the role of the Holy Spirit and function more like a medium rather than as a true prophet. There is only "one mediator between God and mankind, the man Christ Jesus" (1 Timothy 2:5). True prophets announce the words of God in such a way that we fall down and worship Him, and then the Holy Spirit guides each of God's children—not human agents who function like mediums between God and His children.

What was the major function of a prophet?

Why might a message from a genuine prophet be uncomfortable for believers in a church?

How do false prophets attempt to manipulate people?

What would you do if someone said, "God told me to tell you . . ."? Would you receive it, question it, or rebuke it? Why?

How could you discern a false prophet or teacher?

_____

_____

_____

He will judge false prophets, who have not received the gift of prophecy from God. They are not possessed of the fear of God, either. Instead, either for the sake of vainglory, or with a view to some personal advantage (or acting in some other way under the influence of a wicked spirit), they pretend to utter prophecies, while all the time they lie against God.

Irenaeus (AD 130–202)

3

Signs and Wonders

Deuteronomy 13:1–18

Key Point

The apostles performed signs and wonders, but so will false prophets and messiahs.

Key Verse

The apostles performed many signs and wonders among the people.

Acts 5:12

Jesus performed many miracles during His public ministry, and "the apostles performed many signs and wonders among the people" (Acts 5:12). The occurrence of a sign or wonder reveals supernatural presence, but that presence may not always be God. Speaking of the latter days, Jesus said, "False messiahs and false prophets will appear and perform signs and miracles to deceive, if possible, even the elect. So be on your guard; I have told you everything ahead of time" (Mark 13:22–23).

Ever since the Fall, false prophets have plagued God's chosen people and caused them to go after other gods. Moses wrote that for a prophet to be true, what he said would happen must come to pass (see Deuteronomy 18:20–22). Prophets were to be put to death if they spoke presumptuously. However, what about false prophets who performed signs and wonders and they came to pass, *but their message was to follow other gods?* Another test mentioned in Deuteronomy addressed this issue.

This was a test for God's people to find out whether they loved Him with all their hearts and all their souls (see Deuteronomy 13:1–3). Such false prophets who failed these tests were to be stoned to death, and it was to be members of their family who carried out the death sentence (see verses 5–10). Either the prediction was wrong, or the message was wrong, but the latter was most offensive.

False prophets could pollute an entire city. In such situations, the whole city was to be annihilated (see Deuteronomy 13:12–15). Obviously, the world has not followed this law, or huge numbers of people and people groups would have been wiped out. The Church has no mandate to stone false prophets, but these Old Testament passages reveal how serious we must take the warning that there will be false prophets who will "prove themselves" by signs and wonders.

There is no question that Satan and his demons can perform signs and wonders, and there is no question that the occult works. The real question is whether the supernatural acts lead people toward or away from the one true God. Quack doctors, shamans, psychics, and New Age practitioners can come under the spell of evil spirits and channel information about people and events that appears to be accurate. Undiscerning people can be easily impressed by their spiritual insights and might assume they are getting good spiritual direction. When the undiscerning receive guidance through the occult, they usually don't know they are following other gods.

The level of deception will intensify before the Lord returns. In Paul's second letter to the Thessalonians, he warns them not to allow anyone to deceive them into thinking that the day of the Lord had already arrived. The Lord won't return until there has been a falling away from the faith and the man of lawlessness is revealed (see 2 Thessalonians 2:3). The man of lawlessness is probably the Antichrist of Revelation 13, and he will proclaim himself to be God (see 2 Thessalonians 2:4). "The coming of the lawless one will be in accordance with how Satan works. He will use all sorts of displays of power through signs and wonders that serve the lie, and all the ways that wickedness deceives those who are perishing. They perish because they refused to love the truth and so be saved" (2 Thessalonians 2:9–10).

What does the presence of signs and wonders signify? What doesn't it signify?

By what two criteria can we evaluate a prophet?

Is the general public generally gullible or skeptical? Why?

Are you generally gullible or skeptical about signs and wonders? Who or what influenced you in that direction?

What concerns do you have about yourself and your church in these latter days about counterfeit spirituality? Do you have the ability to discern?

_____

_____

_____

"And his coming is according to the working of Satan with all power and signs and lying wonders" [2 Thessalonians 2:9]. This means that Satan will use him [the lawless one] as his personal instrument. Realizing that his own condemnation will no longer be deferred, he will no longer wage war through his ministers in his usual way, but now openly, in person. "With all signs and lying wonders," for the father of falsehood will display his lying works and cheating fantasies, to make the people think they see a dead man raised, when he is not raised, and the lame walking, and the blind receiving sight, when there are no such cures.

Cyril of Jerusalem (AD 313–386)

4

Counterfeits Within the Church

2 Peter 2:1–10

Key Point

False prophets and teachers have a rebellious spirit and will secretly introduce destructive heresies.

Key Verse

He must also have a good reputation with outsiders, so that he will not fall into disgrace and into the devil's trap.

1 Timothy 3:7

Federal agents who are assigned to catch counterfeiters spend the bulk of their time studying real currency, not counterfeit currency. The more familiar they are with the real thing, the easier it is for them to spot the counterfeit. In the same way, our focus is to know the Lord and understand His ways. That is the primary means by which our churches can detect false prophets and teachers and become cult-proof. Being a discerning Christian who knows the truth is critical, because false prophets and teachers will arise from among us and "secretly introduce destructive heresies, even denying the sovereign Lord who bought them" (2 Peter 2:1). These servants of Satan will be disguised as ministers of righteousness and will profess to be Christians (see 2 Corinthians 11:15).

The Holy Spirit works to unite the Church, but false prophets and teachers seek to divide it. The Holy Spirit leads people into all truth, but the truth is not in these people. They can't be identified by asking them to sign a doctrinal statement, because they have no problem lying. Many believers will follow their shameful ways, and the truth will be maligned. Their followers will be captivated by their looks, personality, charm, and charisma, but these are not the biblical criteria by which we validate a ministry or minister. The biblical standards are truth and righteousness, both of which are maligned by false teachers.

Peter identifies two primary ways that we can identify false prophets and teachers who operate within the Church. First, they will eventually reveal their immorality by following the corrupt desire of their sinful nature (see 2 Peter 2:10). It is not likely that their immorality will be easy to spot at first, but it will eventually surface in their lives. They are con artists who work under the cover of darkness and do not want their deeds to be exposed. Second, they despise authority (see verse 10). They have an independent spirit. They won't answer to anyone, and they are critical of those who are over them. They set up smoke screens to keep attention away from themselves, and they put everyone else on the defensive.

Once they have sown their seeds of destruction in the Church, they are difficult to remove. If we try to remove the sons of the evil one, we may root up the children of God with them (see Matthew 13:29). That is why we must be so careful about whom we ordain into ministry or ask to serve as elders and deacons. Paul gives the requirements for Christian leadership in 1 Timothy 3:1–13 and Titus 1:5–9, and they are all related to godly character. Although nobody is perfect, these are the standards to which we are to aspire. People should be disqualified if they appeal to a different standard or fail to exhibit the fruit of the Spirit. Being popular, smart, wealthy, influential, politically savvy, talented, and clever are qualities the world may esteem, but they are not included in the requirements to be a spiritual leader. We need to remember to look for godliness above all else in those we are considering to promote to leadership roles.

What is the best way to detect a counterfeit?

_____

_____

_____

What are the two primary ways that false prophets and teachers can be identified?

_____

_____

_____

Why is it so hard to remove the effects of false prophets once they have been allowed to sow their seeds of discord?

_____

_____

_____

How can you detect a rebellious spirit?

_____

_____

_____

What kinds of leaders do you look up to? Is that because of their abilities or because of their character—that is, because of who they are or what they can do?

_____

_____

_____

The way of truth will be blasphemed by the heretics not only in those people whom they manage to win over to their errors but also in those who reject Christianity by the wicked things which they see these heretics doing, and because they know no better, imagine that all Christians must be caught up in the same depravity.

Bede (AD 673–735)

5

Testing the Spirits

1 John 3:21–4:6

Key Point

Behind every prophetic utterance is the Holy Spirit or an evil spirit, which is why we are told to test the spirits.

Key Verses

Do not quench the Spirit. Do not treat prophecies with contempt but test them all; hold on to what is good, reject every kind of evil.

1 Thessalonians 5:19–22

Jesus said, "By their fruit you will recognize them" (Matthew 7:16). To bear fruit, we have to abide in Christ and walk by the Spirit. John said, "This is how we know who the children of God are and who the children of the devil are: Anyone who does not do what is right is not God's child, nor is anyone who does not love their brother and sister" (1 John 3:10). Living a righteous life, bearing fruit, and loving our neighbor as ourselves are the marks of a true believer.

Christians know that Christ lives within them by the Spirit that He gave them. That is not the case for false prophets, which is why we are to "not believe every spirit, but to test the spirits to see whether they are from God" (4:1). It takes as much spiritual maturity to *not* believe every spirit as it does to believe in the one true God. The discerning believer finds the balance between superstition that believes everything and suspicion that believes nothing.

True prophets are the mouthpiece of the "Spirit of God" (verse 2). False prophets are the mouthpieces of the "spirit of falsehood" (verse 6) or "the spirit of the antichrist" (verse 3). False prophets have no problem lying, which is why we need to test the spirit, not the person. "Every spirit that acknowledges that Jesus Christ has come in the flesh is from God" (1 John 4:2).

The confession that Jesus came in the flesh goes beyond acknowledging Jesus as the Messiah; it is a public profession of faith in Christ as Lord and Savior that is spoken openly and boldly. Evil spirits recognized Jesus during His public ministry, but they did not confess Him as Lord. Paul wrote, "Therefore I want you to know that no one who is speaking by the Spirit of God says, 'Jesus be cursed,' and no one can say, 'Jesus is Lord,' except by the Holy Spirit" (1 Corinthians 12:3). Demons will say that Jesus is Lord, but they will not say Jesus is *their* Lord.

A young man who had once been heralded as a prophet and gave prophetic messages in churches was now under psychiatric care. When asked how he received his prophetic "gift," he said, "I received it after someone helped me receive the gift of tongues." We don't help other people receive gifts—God gives them as He wishes. The man was willing to have the gift tested, and while speaking in tongues the spirit was asked, "In obedience to Scripture, are you the Holy Spirit of God?" Suddenly a voice came from the young man, saying, "I am He."

The spirit was then asked, "Are you the Spirit of Christ who came in the flesh, was crucified, and raised again to sit at the right hand of the Father?" The response was, "No, not He." Wrong spirit! "Every spirit that does not acknowledge Jesus is not from God" (verse 3). "We are from God, and whoever knows God listens to us; but whoever is not from God does not listen to us. This is how we recognize the Spirit of truth and the spirit of falsehood" (verse 6).

What are the marks of a true believer in Christ?

_____

_____

_____

What is the difference between testing the spirit and testing the person?

_____

_____

_____

Can one test the spirit if it is not being manifested?

_____

_____

_____

What would you have done when the spirit spoke through the young man, saying, "I am He"? How can you discern what Spirit is holy and what spirit is wicked?

_____

_____

_____

How do you strike the balance between superstition (believing everything) and suspicion (believing nothing)?

_____

_____

_____

Just as in ancient Israel there were some prophets who spoke the word of God and others who did not, so also, as soon as the apostles appeared, speaking in Christ and having the Holy Spirit whom the Lord had given to them, many false apostles were sent by the devil to counterfeit the teaching of the gospel. It is essential to have the gift of the Holy Spirit, which is called the discernment of spirits, in order to have the ability to test the spirits, to see which ones are to be believed, and which ones are to be rejected.

Didymus the Blind (AD 313–398)

Degrees of Spiritual Vulnerability

The woman who sent the following testimony initially came to see me about her friend who had a spiritual problem. She did not even realize she had a spiritual problem of her own. I told her that she needed to go through the Steps to Freedom in Christ before she tried to help her friend, and she was agreeable.

I suffered a lifetime of sexual, physical, and verbal abuse. I lived off and on with mentally unstable parents who suffered from schizophrenia (my father) and dissociative identity disorder (my mother). I was thrown into foster care and tossed from one family to another. I struggled with rejection as each family complained I was too difficult to handle. I entered my teen years rebelling and experimenting with drugs, witchcraft, and sex. Then I met my Savior at the age of twenty-two. I committed my life to Him and fought to turn my struggling marriage around.

When I became a Christian, I turned over my self-destructive behaviors, which was a real battle. I struggled with condemning, anxious, depressing, and every other kind of negative thoughts from dawn to dusk. I would even awake at night with my failures hanging over my head—a non-stop barrage of mental torment. I could not have any lasting relationships, because I believed everyone else had the same negative belief about me that I had about myself.

Ten years of marriage and four beautiful girls later, God arranged for me to be led through the Steps to Freedom in Christ. I knew this was my moment to let go of everything that had haunted me, but it was so much more than that. At the end of the session, I was asked to close my eyes and relate what I was experiencing mentally. I could hardly believe it—my mind was quiet! There were no more negative thoughts. The constant barrage of negative thinking that had haunted me for years suddenly ended. My head felt empty and the room seemed lighter, as though somebody had turned on another light. It was amazing and liberating!

I had never had such mental peace like that before. Just a few hours earlier I had believed that those "thoughts" were normal and just something I had to put up with. It was an amazing thing to actually be free from them. Thank you, God, for setting me free. I do not live in fear that those thoughts will return. Now I recognize them for what they are; spiritual oppression from the enemy. I know he wants me to believe his lies, but I will never willingly give him that opportunity again. I belong to the Lord Jesus Christ. I want people to know that there is true freedom to be experienced in Christ our Lord. God can be trusted.

Like this woman, many Christians have no idea how much bondage they are in until they find their freedom through genuine repentance. There are some ministries that believe that Christians can't have spiritual problems. So what would they do to help this lady? Other ministries don't go quite that far but deem many of these victims as being unsaved.

Some ministries believe there is no need to deal with anything in our past, because it was all taken care of at the cross. Usually that is said by someone who doesn't want to deal with his or her own issues, and what that person is saying is half true. God has done all that is necessary for us to live a free and productive life in Christ, but we need to repent and believe the whole gospel. You haven't repented if you haven't renounced past cultic and occultic practices as well as deceptive lies; or forgiven people in your past; or dealt with your pride and rebellion; or renounced the sexual uses of your body as an instrument of unrighteousness that allowed sin to reign in your mortal body.

To what degree are true believers vulnerable? The first concern of our Lord in the High Priestly Prayer in John 17 is that we be kept from the evil one. Obviously, Jesus believed we have some degree of vulnerability. The big question that weighs on many believers' minds is whether a Christian can be demon-possessed.

Daily Readings

1. Demon Possession	Mark 5:1–20
2. Spiritual Bondage	Luke 13:10–17
3. Loss of Control	Luke 22:31–34
4. Spiritual Cleansing	1 Corinthians 5:1–13
5. A Good Ending	Revelation 19:1–10

1

Demon Possession

Mark 5:1–20

Key Point

Liberated Christians are clothed in Christ and right-minded.

Key Verse

When they came to Jesus, they saw the man who had been possessed by the legion of demons, sitting there, dressed and in his right mind; and they were afraid.

Mark 5:15

The story of the Gadarene demoniac (see Mark 5:1–20 NKJV) is the worst case of demon possession recorded in the New Testament. No person was able to physically control this man, but spiritually he was no match for Jesus, who demonstrated His authority over demons. The term "demon possessed" is the English translation for the single Greek word *daimonizomai* (verb) or *daimonizomenos* (participle)—which is best transliterated as "demonized."

To be "demonized" means to be under the control of one or more demons. The term never occurs in the Epistles, so we have no way of knowing how it would apply to believers in the Church Age. Possession implies ownership, and we do know that Satan and his demons cannot have or own a Christian who belongs to God. In that regard, as Christians, we are possessed by the Holy Spirit. We have been purchased by the blood of the Lord Jesus Christ and we belong to Him. But that does not mean that we are not vulnerable. If we open the door to Satan's influence, he will invade and claim squatter's rights. He will resist eviction until the ground beneath him is removed through repentance and faith in God.

Another Greek phrase in the Gospels is *echein daimonion*, which means to "have a demon." The religious leaders used this phrase when they accused both John the Baptist and Jesus of being demonized (see Luke 7:33; John 7:20). The Pharisees made these accusations because they knew that John and Jesus' supernatural knowledge had to have been communicated to them through some spiritual means. It was common in those days to have esoteric knowledge communicated by demons through human agents (mediums and spiritists). The Pharisees were unwilling to recognize Jesus as the Messiah, so they wrongly assumed that the source of his information was from demons instead of God.

Some people make the theological argument that the Holy Spirit and an evil spirit cannot coexist in a Christian in order to make the argument that Christians cannot be invaded by demons. However, that argument does not stand up for several reasons. First, Satan is the prince of this world and the "ruler of the kingdom of the air" (Ephesians 2:2). Thus, Satan and his demons are present in the atmosphere of this world, and so is the omnipresent Holy Spirit—which means they *do* coexist.

Second, Satan still has access to God the Father in heaven (see Revelation 12:10). Third, the Holy Spirit is in union—in coexistence—with our human spirit, and surely we don't consider our human spirit perfect. Fourth, spatial arguments don't apply to the spiritual realm, for there are no natural barriers or physical boundaries for spirits. This is why we shouldn't think of a church building as a sanctuary. Our sanctuary is "in Christ," not some physical, man-made structure. Fifth, if we are paying attention to a deceiving spirit, the spirit's presence cannot be external only. The battle is in the mind.

If it were true that an evil spirit and the Holy Spirit could not operate at the same time and in the same sphere, there would be no need for the Bible to command us to be alert and put on the armor of God. The purpose of armor is to stop penetration, and that is for the protection of the believer, not the unbeliever.

What does it mean to be "demonized"?

_____

_____

_____

Why did the religious leaders accuse Jesus and John the Baptist of having a demon?

_____

_____

_____

Does the Holy Spirit and evil spirits presently coexist on earth? Why or why not?

_____

_____

_____

Can you come under the influence of one or more demons? If yes, how?

_____

_____

_____

What do you think it means that the demonized man was "in his right mind"?

_____

_____

_____

[Jesus] did this so that you might know that the demons would have done the same thing to human beings and would have drowned them if God had allowed them to do so. But he restrained the demons, stopped them, and allowed them to do no such thing. When their power was transferred to the swine, it became clear to all witnesses what they would have done to persons. From this we learn that if the demons had the power to possess swine, they could also have possessed humans.

John Chrysostom (AD 347–407)

2

Spiritual Bondage

Luke 13:10–17

Key Point

Recognizing our spiritual vulnerability keeps up our defenses and enables a wholistic answer for life's problems.

Key Verse

You, dear children, are from God and have overcome them, because the one who is in you is greater than the one who is in the world.

1 John 4:4

There are two critical reasons why we must acknowledge our spiritual vulnerability. First, if we adopt the attitude that Christians are somehow immune to Satan's attack, we actually become defenseless. There would be no need to put on the armor of God, be alert, or take every thought captive. Paul urged the church at Corinth, "Forgive . . . in order that Satan might not outwit us. For we are not unaware of his schemes" (2 Corinthians 2:10–11). Christians aren't immune, they're the target; and ignorance isn't bliss, its defeat. One can bury his or her head in the sand like an ostrich, but that leaves a huge target exposed.

Second, if we are ignorant of our spiritual vulnerability, we cannot correctly diagnosis many mental, emotional, and even physical problems. Therefore, we don't have a comprehensive answer. Attributing Satan's activities to the flesh, which is a common error in the Western church, leads only to self-condemnation and defeat. On the other hand, blaming the devil for our own carnal nature is a lame excuse and just as defeating. We have to crucify the flesh and grow out of our old flesh patterns, and we must resist the devil so that he will flee from us. We don't grow out of spiritual attacks, nor do we exercise our spiritual authority by telling the flesh to leave. We have to know the nature of our problem in order to have the right answer.

Satan kept a "daughter of Abraham" (Luke 13:16) in bondage for eighteen years. She was a believer under the Old Covenant who was worshiping God in a synagogue—a God-fearing woman who was under spiritual bondage. As soon as Jesus released her from spiritual bondage, her physical problem was cured. This passage clearly indicates that Satan can affect a person physically. Twenty-five percent of those whom Jesus delivered from demons in the Gospel of Mark experienced a physical healing. That doesn't even take into account all the psychosomatic illnesses that were cured when people became mentally and emotionally free. Obviously, not all our physical problems are caused by demons, but Scripture allows for the fact that some are.

One of the more intriguing illustrations is Paul's "thorn in the flesh." Almost every Christian has heard of it, but few know what it was, even though the passage tells us. "I was given a thorn in my flesh, a messenger of Satan, to torment me" (2 Corinthians 12:7). A messenger of Satan is a demon. One time, a co-ed at a Christian university wanted "power perfected in weakness," so she prayed and asked for a "thorn in the flesh." She started to have symptoms of multiple sclerosis and was even diagnosed with it until she confided with a professor who informed her what the "thorn in the flesh" was. When she renounced it, the symptoms disappeared.

James teaches that the result of yielding to jealousy and selfish ambition results in a "wisdom" that is earthly, natural, and demonic (see 3:14–16). In Ephesians 4:26–27, Paul writes, "'In your anger do not sin': Do not let the sun go down while you are still angry, and do not give the devil a foothold." The word "foothold" in this passage literally means "place," so Paul is saying that we can allow the devil a place in our lives if we fail to speak the truth in love and be emotionally honest.

What is the result of falsely identifying the flesh as the culprit when it is primarily a spiritual problem?

_____

_____

_____

Why don't Christians in the western Church often know what Paul's "thorn in the flesh" was?

_____

_____

_____

If people are paying attention to a deceiving spirit and believing lies, how will that affect how they feel? Could it eventually affect one physically, as in psychosomatic illnesses?

_____

_____

_____

Why do you think God allowed a demon to become a thorn in the flesh for Paul? (Note: it also tells us that in the passage.)

_____

_____

_____

Does it scare you to know that you may be spiritually vulnerable? Or does it cause you to be more alert and engaged and give you hope for resolving a lot of issues that you couldn't before? Explain.

_____

_____

_____

The right to tempt a man is granted to the devil . . . whether God or the devil initiates the plan or for the purpose of the judgment of a sinner, who is handed over to the devil as to an executioner. This was the case with Saul. "The spirit of the Lord departed from Saul, and an evil spirit from the Lord troubled and stifled him" [1 Samuel 16:14]. Again, it may happen in order to humble a man, as St. Paul tells us that there was given to him a thorn, a messenger of Satan, to buffet him, and even this sort of thing is not permitted for the humiliation of holy men through torment of the flesh, unless it be done so that their power to resist may be perfected in weakness.

Tertullian (AD 160–220)

3

Loss of Control

Luke 22:31–34

Key Point

Giving in to pride can make believers susceptible to Satan's snares.

Key Verse

Then [Jesus] touched their eyes and said, "According to your faith let it be done to you."

Matthew 9:29

Jesus said, "Simon, Simon, behold, Satan has demanded permission to sift you like wheat" (Luke 22:31 NASB). On what basis could Satan have demanded this right? The context indicates that pride may have been the grounds for Satan's request. "A dispute also arose among them [the disciples] as to which of them was considered to be greatest" (verse 24). God had kicked Satan out of heaven because of his pride (see Isaiah 14:12; Luke 10:18). Satan was demanding that God do the same for Peter.

Notice how Jesus responded to Satan's request: "But I have prayed for you, Simon, that your faith may not fail. And when you have turned back, strengthen your brothers" (verse 32). Jesus did not say that He would prevent

Satan from having his way with Peter. Peter responded that he was ready to die or go to prison for Jesus (see verse 33). In spite of his attitude, Jesus said Peter would deny Him three times (see verse 34), which Peter later did. Peter had lost some measure of control in his life because of pride, and Jesus prayed for his successful recovery from it. The devil didn't make Peter do it—Peter denied Jesus because in his pride he allowed himself to become vulnerable.

No Christian can ever say "the devil made me do it," because we are all responsible for our own attitudes and actions. Satan simply takes advantage of the opportunities we give to him. We have all the resources and protection we need to live victorious lives in Christ, but when we leave a door open for the devil by not resisting temptation, accusation, and deception, he will enter. We won't lose our salvation, but giving ground to the enemy will affect our daily victory.

The army that goes to war unprepared will suffer terrible casualties. If we as Christians fail to use our armor, Satan will not stop short of invading our citadel. He will take us captive to do his will (see 2 Timothy 2:26). The world, the flesh, and the devil are continually at war against the life of the Spirit within us. If we use our bodies as instruments of unrighteousness, we will allow sin to reign in our mortal bodies (see Romans 6:12–14). If we fail to take every thought captive to the obedience of Christ (see 2 Corinthians 10:5), we will end up being deceived. If we fail to forgive from our hearts, Jesus Himself will turn us over to the tormentors (see Matthew 18:34–35).

Choosing truth, living a righteous life, and donning the armor of God are a believer's individual responsibility. We have a responsibility to one another, but not for one another. If a believer chooses to go into this world without his or her armor on, that believer will suffer consequences. As much as that may be a matter of concern for us, we still cannot make those decisions for others or assume their responsibility.

On what basis could Satan have demanded to sift Peter as wheat?

Can believers ever rightly say "the devil made me do it"? Why or why not?

We may surrender some control of our lives through our own actions and attitudes, but do we ever cease being who we are in Christ? Why or why not?

Generally speaking, why do you think the Church speaks out against the sins of the flesh but says little about pride and bitterness? Which do you think is worse?

Why should you consider the seriousness of pride, arrogance, and self-sufficiency?

"Awake and watch" is one of the holy apostles' summons to us. The net of sin is spread everywhere, and Satan makes his prey in different ways. He grabs hold of us by many passions and leads us on to a condemned mind. . . . The disciples had given in to human weakness and were arguing with one another who was the leader and superior of the rest.

Cyril of Alexandria (AD 376–444)

4

Spiritual Cleansing

1 Corinthians 5:1–13

Key Point

Church discipline must be tough enough to ensure purity but tender enough to set captives free and restore them to Christian fellowship.

Key Verses

Husbands, love your wives, just as Christ loved the church and gave himself up for her to make her holy, cleansing her by the washing with water through the word, and to present her to himself as a radiant church, without stain or wrinkle or any other blemish, but holy and blameless.

Ephesians 5:25–27

Paul's first letter to the church at Corinth reveals that he was appalled by the lack of spiritual discipline in that body of believers (see 1 Corinthians 5:1). A man was having an incestuous relationship with his father's wife (see verse 1). He had been so deluded by Satan and so controlled by immorality that he apparently flaunted his illicit relationship before the whole church (see verse 2).

Paul's judgment on the matter was severe: "Hand this man over to Satan for the destruction of the flesh, so that his spirit may be saved on the day of the Lord" (verse 5). Paul thought it best in this situation to allow Satan to have his way with the man in hopes that he would finally say "I've had enough" and repent. God is not above using Satan to discipline us if that is what it takes to bring about repentance. Satan is tethered by the permissive will of God and can only do that which is permitted by Him.

Expelling the man from the church was Paul's way of handing him over to Satan. In the world, he would be severed from the church and the power of Christ. The world was Satan's territory, and the man would have to suffer the consequences of his sins without the spiritual protection of the local church. The church was not meant to be a gathering place for sexually immoral believers. In fact, believers in the Early Church were to expel the wicked from their fellowship (see 1 Corinthians 5:13). Otherwise, these spiritually bound people would contaminate the church with the wrong spirit, and some would undoubtedly become sexual predators and defile others.

God is more concerned about the Church's purity than He is about the Church's growth, because church growth is dependent on church purity. The Holy Spirit is working in our midst to present the Bride of Christ "as a radiant church, without stain or wrinkle or any other blemish, but holy and blameless" (Ephesians 5:27). If the wrong spirit controls professing believers and they in turn are controlling the Church, then the wrong spirit is controlling the Church. For the local church, this means that just one unruly child can disrupt a family, a Christian camp, or a Sunday School, and just one immoral, bitter, or deceived adult can disrupt a board or church meeting. That is why church discipline is so necessary.

When do we stop trying to nurture a bad apple back to health and get rid of the apple before the whole barrel is defiled? That is one of the most difficult decisions that spiritual leaders have to make when seeking to ensure that the local church is under the lordship of Christ. The first priority is to carry out the ministry of reconciliation. If that should fail, the next priority is to expel from our fellowships those with a wrong spirit. We need to do this so that many others will not be defiled.

A growing church survives in an atmosphere of grace and in the context of trusting relationships. That makes the church vulnerable to those who would prey on the good natures of committed believers. Discipline is a proof of our love, which must be tough enough to ensure church purity but tender enough to set captives free and restore them to Christian fellowship.

What was Paul's instruction to the church at Corinth on how to deal with the man living in an incestuous relationship?

What was Paul's intention by having the man expelled from the church?

What negative effect can undisciplined believers have on a church?

How far would you go to help another believer who was having a negative effect on your Bible study, class, or church before you removed him or her?

Do you think church discipline is a matter for the leaders only, or do you have some responsibility in restoring a fellow believer? Explain.

_____

_____

_____

Just as the sin of one person contaminates many if it is not dealt with once it is known, so also does the sin of the many who know what is happening and either do not turn away from it or pretend that they have not noticed. Sin does not look like sin if it is not corrected or avoided by anybody.

Ambrosiaster (written c. AD 366–384)

5

A Good Ending

Revelation 19:1–10

Key Point

God makes everything right in the end.

Key Verse

And the devil, who deceived them, was thrown into the lake of burning sulfur, where the beast and the false prophet had been thrown. They will be tormented day and night for ever and ever.

Revelation 20:10

History is *His Story*, which is where we began the VICTORY SERIES. Like any good novel, you want to skip to the end of the book to see how it all works out, and that is especially true if you are in His story. Sometimes you wonder in the heat of battle whether your side is going to win. You don't have to wonder, because God has revealed what happens in the end. You win! Your name is written in the Lamb's Book of Life, and Satan is thrown into the lake of fire. Until then, take your place in Christ, keep the faith, and fight the good fight. Finish this study by verbally declaring your identity and position "in Christ" as follows:

I renounce the lie that I am rejected, unloved, or shameful. In Christ:

I am God's child	John 1:12
I am Jesus' chosen friend	John 15:15
I have been made holy and am accepted by God (justified)	Romans 5:1
I am united with the Lord and one with Him in spirit	1 Corinthians 6:17
I have been bought with a price—I belong to God	1 Corinthians 6:20
I am a member of Christ's body, a part of His family	1 Corinthians 12:27
I am a saint, a holy one	Ephesians 1:1
I have been adopted as God's child	Ephesians 1:5
I have direct access to God through the Holy Spirit	Ephesians 2:18
I have been bought back (redeemed) and forgiven of all my sins	Colossians 1:14
I am complete in Christ	Colossians 2:10

I renounce the lie that I am guilty, unprotected, alone, or abandoned. In Christ:

I am free forever from punishment (condemnation)	Romans 8:1–2
I am assured that all things work together for good	Romans 8:28
I am free from any condemning charges against me	Romans 8:31
I cannot be separated from the love of God	Romans 8:35
I have been established, anointed, and sealed by God	2 Corinthians 1:21–22
I am hidden with Christ in God	Colossians 3:3
I am sure that the good work God has started in me will be finished	Philippians 1:6
I am a citizen of heaven	Philippians 3:20
I have not been given a spirit of fear but of power, love, and self-discipline	2 Timothy 1:7
I can find grace and mercy in time of need	Hebrews 4:16
I am born of God and the evil one cannot touch me	1 John 5:18

I renounce the lie that I am worthless, inadequate, helpless, or hopeless. In Christ:

I am the salt and light for everyone around me	Matthew 5:13–15
I am a part of the true vine—joined to Christ and able to produce much fruit	John 15:1, 5
I have been handpicked by Jesus to bear fruit	John 15:16
I am a personal witness of Christ's	Acts 1:8
I am God's temple where the Holy Spirit lives	1 Corinthians 3:16
I am at peace with God and He has given me the work of making peace between Himself and other people—I am a minister of reconciliation	2 Corinthians 5:17
I am God's co-worker	2 Corinthians 6:1
I am seated with Christ in the heavenlies	Ephesians 2:6
I am God's workmanship	Ephesians 2:10
I may approach God with freedom and confidence	Ephesians 3:12
I can do all things through Christ who strengthens me	Philippians 4:13

The grace of our Creator is so great that He has allowed us both to know Him and to love Him, and moreover, to love Him as children love a wonderful Father. It would be no small thing if we were able to love God in the way that a servant loves his master or a worker his employer. But loving God as Father is much greater still.

Bede (AD 673–735)

Leader's Tips

The following are some guidelines for leaders to follow when using the VICTORY SERIES studies with a small group. Generally, the ideal size for a group is between 10 and 20 people, which is small enough for meaningful fellowship but large enough for dynamic group interaction. It is typically best to stop opening up the group to members after the second session and invite them to join the next study after the six weeks are complete.

Structuring Your Time Together

For best results, ensure that all participants have a copy of the book. They should be encouraged to read the material and consider the questions and applications on their own before the group session. If participants have to miss a meeting, they should keep abreast of the study on their own. The group session reinforces what they learned and offers the valuable perspectives of others. Learning best takes place in the context of committed relationships, so do more than just share answers. Take the time to care and share with one another. You might want to use the first week to distribute material and give everyone a chance to tell others who they are.

If you discussed just one topic a week, it would take several years to finish the VICTORY SERIES. If you did five a week, it is possible to complete the whole series in 48 weeks. All the books in the series were written with a six-week study in mind. However, each group is different and each will have to discover its own pace. If too many participants come unprepared, you may have to read, or at least summarize, the text before discussing the questions and applications.

It would be great if this series was used for a church staff or Bible study at work and could be done one topic at a time, five days a week. However, most study groups will likely be meeting weekly. It is best to start with a time of sharing and prayer for one another. Start with the text or Bible passage for each topic and move to the discussion questions and application. Take time at the end to summarize what has been covered, and dismiss in prayer.

Group Dynamics

Getting a group of people actively involved in discussing critical issues of the Christian life is very rewarding. Not only does group interaction help to create interest, stimulate thinking, and encourage effective learning, but it is also vital for building quality relationships within the group. Only as people begin to share their thoughts and feelings will they begin to build bonds of friendship and support.

It is important to set some guidelines at the beginning of the study, as follows:

- There are no wrong questions.
- Everyone should feel free to share his or her ideas without recrimination.
- Focus on the issues and not on personalities.
- Try not to dominate the discussions or let others do so.
- Personal issues shared in the group must remain in the group.
- Avoid gossiping about others in or outside the group.
- Side issues should be diverted to the end of the class for those who wish to linger and discuss them further.
- Above all, help each other grow in Christ.

Some may find it difficult to share with others, and that is okay. It takes time to develop trust in any group. A leader can create a more open and sharing atmosphere by being appropriately vulnerable himself or herself. A good leader doesn't have all the answers and doesn't need to for this study. Some questions raised are extremely difficult to answer and have been puzzled over for years by educated believers. We will never have all the answers to every question in this age, but that does not preclude discussion over eternal matters. Hopefully, it will cause some to dig deeper.

Leading the Group

The following tips can be helpful in making group interaction a positive learning opportunity for everyone:

- When a question or comment is raised that is off the subject, suggest that you will bring it up again at the end of the class if anyone is still interested.

- When someone talks too much, direct a few questions specifically to other people, making sure not to put any shy people on the spot. Talk privately with the "dominator" and ask for cooperation in helping to draw out the quieter group members.

- Hopefully the participants have already written their answers to the discussion questions and will share that when asked. If most haven't come prepared, give them some time to personally reflect on what has been written and the questions asked.

- If someone asks a question that you don't know how to answer, admit it and move on. If the question calls for insight about personal experience, invite group members to comment. If the question requires specialized knowledge, offer to look for an answer before the next session. (Make sure to follow up the next session.)

- When group members disagree with you or each other, remind them that it is possible to disagree without becoming disagreeable. To help clarify the issues while maintaining a climate of mutual acceptance, encourage those on opposite sides to restate what they have heard the other person(s) saying about the issue. Then invite each side to evaluate how accurately they feel their position was presented. Ask group members to identify as many points as possible related to the topic on which both sides agree, and then lead the group in examining

153

other Scriptures related to the topic, looking for common ground that they can all accept.

• Finally, urge group members to keep an open heart and mind and a willingness to continue loving one another while learning more about the topic at hand.

If the disagreement involves an issue on which your church has stated a position, be sure that stance is clearly and positively presented. This should be done not to squelch dissent but to ensure that there is no confusion over where your church stands.

Notes

Session Four: Overcoming Accusation

1. Bob Benson, *Laughter in the Walls* (Nashville: Impact Books, 1996), pp. 80–81.

Chapter 1: The Accuser

1. Neil T. Anderson, Rich Miller, Paul Travis, *Breaking the Bondage of Legalism* (Eugene, OR: Harvest House, 2003), pp. 9–10.

Session Five: Overcoming Deception

1. The Catechism of the Catholic Church, part I, section 2, article 9, no. 857.

Victory Series Scope and Sequence Overview

The VICTORY SERIES is composed of eight studies that create a comprehensive discipleship course. Each study builds on the previous one and provides six sessions of material. These can be used by an individual or in a small group setting. There are leader's tips at the back of each study for those leading a small group.

The following scope and sequence overview gives a brief summary of the content of each of the eight studies in the VICTORY SERIES. Some studies also include articles related to the content of that study.

The Victory Series

Study 1   God's Story for You: Discover the Person God Created You to Be
Session One: The Story of Creation Session Two: The Story of the Fall Session Three: The Story of Salvation Session Four: The Story of God's Sanctification Session Five: The Story of God's Transforming Power Session Six: The Story of God

Study 2   Your New Identity: A Transforming Union With God

Session One: A New Life "in Christ"
Session Two: A New Understanding of God's Character
Session Three: A New Understanding of God's Nature
Session Four: A New Relationship With God
Session Five: A New Humanity
Session Six: A New Beginning

Study 3   Your Foundation in Christ: Live by the Power of the Spirit

Session One: Liberating Truth
Session Two: The Nature of Faith
Session Three: Living Boldly
Session Four: Godly Relationships
Session Five: Freedom of Forgiveness
Session Six: Living by the Spirit

Study 4   Renewing Your Mind: Become More Like Christ

Session One: Being Transformed
Session Two: Living Under Grace
Session Three: Overcoming Anger
Session Four: Overcoming Anxiety
Session Five: Overcoming Depression
Session Six: Overcoming Losses

Study 5   Growing in Christ: Deepen Your Relationship With Jesus

Session One: Spiritual Discernment
Session Two: Spiritual Gifts
Session Three: Growing Through Committed Relationships
Session Four: Overcoming Sexual Bondage
Session Five: Overcoming Chemical Addiction
Session Six: Suffering for Righteousness' Sake

Study 6   Your Life in Christ: Walk in Freedom by Faith

Session One: God's Will
Session Two: Faith Appraisal (Part 1)
Session Three: Faith Appraisal (Part 2)
Session Four: Spiritual Leadership
Session Five: Discipleship Counseling
Session Six: The Kingdom of God

Study 7   Your Authority in Christ: Overcome Strongholds in Your Life

Session One: The Origin of Evil
Session Two: Good and Evil Spirits
Session Three: Overcoming the Opposition
Session Four: Kingdom Sovereignty
Session Five: The Armor of God (Part 1)
Session Six: The Armor of God (Part 2)

Study 8   Your Ultimate Victory: Stand Strong in the Faith

Session One: The Battle for Our Minds
Session Two: The Lure of Knowledge and Power
Session Three: Overcoming Temptation
Session Four: Overcoming Accusation
Session Five: Overcoming Deception
Session Six: Degrees of Spiritual Vulnerability

Books and Resources

Dr. Neil T. Anderson

Core Material

Victory Over the Darkness with study guide, audiobook, and DVD. With over 1,300,000 copies in print, this core book explains who you are in Christ, how to walk by faith in the power of the Holy Spirit, how to be transformed by the renewing of your mind, how to experience emotional freedom, and how to relate to one another in Christ.

The Bondage Breaker with study guide, audiobook, and DVD. With over 1,300,000 copies in print, this book explains spiritual warfare, what our protection is, ways that we are vulnerable, and how we can live a liberated life in Christ.

Breaking Through to Spiritual Maturity. This curriculum teaches the basic message of Freedom in Christ Ministries.

Discipleship Counseling with DVD. This book combines the concepts of discipleship and counseling and teaches the practical integration of theology and psychology for helping Christians resolve their personal and spiritual conflicts through repentance and faith in God.

Steps to Freedom in Christ and interactive video. This discipleship counseling tool helps Christians resolve their personal and spiritual conflicts through genuine repentance and faith in God.

Restored. This book is an expansion of the *Steps to Freedom in Christ*, and offers more explanation and illustrations.

Walking in Freedom. This book is a 21-day devotional that we use for follow-up after leading someone through the Steps to Freedom.

Freedom in Christ is a discipleship course for Sunday school classes and small groups. The course comes with a teacher's guide, a student guide, and a DVD covering 12 lessons and the Steps to Freedom in Christ. This course is designed to enable new and stagnant believers to resolve personal and spiritual conflicts and be established alive and free in Christ.

The Bondage Breaker DVD Experience is also a discipleship course for Sunday school classes and small groups. It is similar to the one above, but the lessons are 15 minutes instead of 30 minutes.

The Daily Discipler. This practical systematic theology is a culmination of all of Dr. Anderson's books covering the major doctrines of the Christian faith and the problems Christians face. It is a five-day-per-week, one-year study that will thoroughly ground believers in their faith.

Specialized Books

The Bondage Breaker, the Next Step. This book has several testimonies of people finding their freedom from all kinds of problems, with commentary by Dr. Anderson. It is an important learning tool for encouragers.

Overcoming Addictive Behavior, with Mike Quarles. This book explores the path to addiction and how a Christian can overcome addictive behaviors.

Overcoming Depression, with Joanne Anderson. This book explores the nature of depression, which is a body, soul, and spirit problem and presents a wholistic answer for overcoming this "common cold" of mental illness.

Liberating Prayer. This book helps believers understand the confusion in their minds when it comes time to pray, and why listening in prayer may be more important than talking.

Daily in Christ, with Joanne Anderson. This popular daily devotional is also being used by thousands of Internet subscribers every day.

Who I Am in Christ. In 36 short chapters, this book describes who you are in Christ and how He meets your deepest needs.

Freedom from Addiction, with Mike and Julia Quarles. Using Mike's testimony, this book explains the nature of chemical addictions and how to overcome them in Christ.

One Day at a Time, with Mike and Julia Quarles. This devotional helps those who struggle with addictive behaviors and explains how to discover the grace of God on a daily basis.

Freedom from Fear, with Rich Miller. This book explains anxiety disorders and how to overcome them.

Setting Your Church Free, with Charles Mylander. This book offers guidelines and encouragement for resolving seemingly impossible corporate conflicts in the church and also provides leaders with a primary means for church growth—releasing the power of God in the church.

Setting Your Marriage Free, with Dr. Charles Mylander. This book explains God's divine plan for marriage and the steps that couples can take to resolve their difficulties.

Christ-Centered Therapy, with Dr. Terry and Julie Zuehlke. This is a textbook explaining the practical integration of theology and psychology for professional counselors.

Getting Anger Under Control, with Rich Miller. This book explains the basis for anger and how to control it.

Grace that Breaks the Chains, with Rich Miller and Paul Travis. This book explains legalism and how to overcome it.

Winning the Battle Within. This book shares God's standards for sexual conduct, the path to sexual addiction, and how to overcome sexual strongholds.

The Path to Reconciliation. God has given the church the ministry of reconciliation. This book explains what that is and how it can be accomplished.

Rough Road to Freedom. This is a book of Dr. Anderson's memoirs.

For more information, contact Freedom In Christ Ministries at the following:

Canada: freedominchrist@sasktel.net or www.ficm.ca

India: isactara@gmail.com

Switzerland: info@freiheitinchristus.ch or www.freiheitinchristus.ch

United Kingdom: info@ficm.org.uk or www.ficm.org.uk

United States: info@ficm.org or www.ficm.org

International: www.ficminternational.org

Dr. Anderson: www.discipleshipcounsel.com

Index

Notes

Notes

Notes

Notes

Notes

Notes

Dr. Neil T. Anderson was formerly the chairman of the Practical Theology Department at Talbot School of Theology. In 1989, he founded Freedom in Christ Ministries, which now has staff and offices in various countries around the world. He is currently on the Freedom in Christ Ministries International Board, which oversees this global ministry. For more information about Dr. Anderson and his ministry, visit his website at www.ficminternational.org.

Also From
Neil T. Anderson

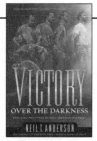

This bestselling landmark book gives you practical, productive ways to discover who you are in Christ. When you realize the power of your true identity, you can shed the burdens of your past, stand against evil influences, and become the person Christ empowers you to be.

Victory Over the Darkness

Great for small group or individual use, these thought-provoking personal reflection questions and applications for each chapter of *Victory Over the Darkness* will help readers grow in the strength and truth of their powerful identity in Jesus Christ.

Victory Over the Darkness Study Guide

◊ BETHANYHOUSE

Stay up-to-date on your favorite books and authors with our free e-newsletters. Sign up today at bethanyhouse.com.

Find us on Facebook. facebook.com/BHPnonfiction

Follow us on Twitter. @bethany_house